Kristi Hugstad's life wasn't just on track, it was a dream: a loving marriage, two beautiful homes and a thriving fitness business she built with her husband Bill.

Until, one day, it all went off the rails.

> *"Bill Brotherton Jr. ran up a graveled embankment in Capistrano Beach, stood on the train tracks that run near the ocean and looked at the engineer of the northbound 808 Metrolink train—arms spread wide..."*

Instead of settling into the life she'd so successfully built, Kristi was left fighting for scraps of hope in a tunnel of inexplicable grief. Once a passionate health and fitness enthusiast, her ambition soon took a more spiritual trajectory – helping others escape the shackles of grief she understood so well.

What I Wish I'd Known shares Kristi's tragic, painful, heart-rending and infinitely hopeful story of love, loss and the strength it takes to start over again. For anyone experiencing loss, Kristi's words are a beacon of light on life's darkest waters.

> *"Grief is not the bewildering territory you want to navigate alone, and Kristi H[illegible] is the best kind of traveling [illegible] hearted, and inspiring.* What I *W[illegible] precisely the kind of field guide anyone in the midst of grieving—whether from an untimely death or any change in life (even the good kind) that brings a sense of loss—will find invaluable."*
>
> —Cathleen Falsani, journalist and author of *The God Factor* and *Sin Boldly*

Morgan James PUBLISHING

Habitat for Humanity® Peninsula and Greater Williamsburg Building Partner

READ TIME: 133min.

SELF-HELP
Death, Grief, Bereavement

ISBN 978-1-68350-365-1
51795
9 781683 503651
$17.95

What I Wish I'd Known

Praise For

WHAT I WISH I'D KNOWN

"Grief is not the bewildering territory you want to navigate alone and Kristi Hugstad is the best kind of traveling companion: candid, openhearted, organized, and inspiring. *What I Wish I'd Known* is precisely the kind of field guide anyone who is in the midst of grieving—whether from an untimely, shocking death or from any kind of change in life (even the good kind) that brings a sense of loss—will find invaluable. Kristi's own story, told with unflinching honesty, is as compelling as it is unforgettable and the way she shares it with her audience instills the sort of trust that is crucial when you're in a dark night of the soul searching for signs of daylight and hope."

—**Cathleen Falsani**, Journalist and
Author of *The God Factor* and *Sin Boldly*

"Grief is painful. And it's personal. How does one pick their way through the path of grief to be healed and find joy again? Our instinct is to withdraw as the pain overwhelms us. Kristi Hugstad, confronted with an enormous loss, ultimately emerged from the darkness to compose a memoir that not only illuminates, but also provides a comforting guide to finding one's way back from the depths of despair."

—**Maurice Possley**, Pulitzer Prize winning Journalist
and *New York Times* Best-Selling Author

"This book, like it's author, is innovative, inspiring, and to the point. Kristi's story has so many components can all relate, from being the victim, to the enabler. Her fresh 'don't think, just do' approach is what makes this book unique. Love she includes examples of what she did to navigate her way through the tunnel of grief. Kudos, Kristi!"

—**Russell Friedman**, Executive Director of
The Grief Recovery Institute

"I only wish I had "What I Wish I'd Known," when I was walking through the fog and depression after the death of some of my close friends and family members. Hugstad knows the pain of grief all too well herself, but has used the experience and knowledge to create a truly useful handbook, if you will, for making it through the most devastating aspects of loss. Practical and uplifting, this book also deepens our understanding of why we are grieving and how to give ourselves time to mourn. I feel like pressing this into the hands of everyone I know, because sooner or later, each of us will need to know its wisdom."

—**Samantha Dunn**, author of *Not By Accident, Faith in Carlos Gomez,* and *Failing Paris*

"Like many of us, I've lost friends and family in the last few years and reading, "What I Wish I'd Known," I discovered new and significant ways to cope with grief. Kristi Hugstad's advice about sleeping on a lost spouse's side of the bed so you don't feel as alone, making sure you have adequate electrolytes such as vitamin D and telling yourself," I have suffered enough, and now it is time to be free," are just a few of the hundreds of ideas she offers in her unique book about finding your path to healing. Kristi's honesty, courage and insight offer truths that can lead all of us to dance in the light."

—**David Whiting**, Metro Columnist, *The Orange County Register*

What I Wish I'd Known

Finding Your Way Through the Tunnel of Grief

Kristi Hugstad

NEW YORK

NASHVILLE • MELBOURNE • VANCOUVER

WHAT I WISH I'D KNOWN

Finding Your Way Through the Tunnel of Grief

Published in New York, New York, by Morgan James Publishing in partnership with Difference Press. Morgan James is a trademark of Morgan James, LLC.
www.MorganJamesPublishing.com

The Morgan James Speakers Group can bring authors to your live event. For more information or to book an event visit The Morgan James Speakers Group at www.TheMorganJamesSpeakersGroup.com.

ISBN 978-1-68350-365-1 paperback
ISBN 978-1-68350-366-8 eBook
Library of Congress Control Number:
2016919217

Cover Design by:
Rachel Lopez
www.r2cdesign.com

Interior Design by:
Bonnie Bushman
The Whole Caboodle Graphic Design

For my sisters, Debbie Davidson and Viki Hugstad,
My niece Tessa Davidson,
And my mom, Val Hugstad,
Who walked with me through my darkest hours.

And in memory of my husband, Bill Brotherton.

Table of Contents

Preface

You've probably picked up this book because you've lost someone you loved very much and are seeking relief; or maybe it's in your hands because you came across it in a bookstore or at a friend's house and you're curious about its contents. Whatever your situation, you'll discover that *What I Wish I'd Known* will get you through any kind of grief you're experiencing.

We tend to think of grief as the natural response to death, but grief encompasses so much more. It's the response to any loss—relationship, job, faith, identity, status, health, your five-year-old daughter's first tooth, the sale of your childhood home. The list goes on and on. Each of us has attached ourselves to something or somebody, and when you lose that special thing or person, you grieve. Always. You can try to run from it all you want, but it will always find you and tackle you when you're not looking.

This is why I wrote *What I Wish I'd Known*. It's my way of helping others deal with their grief head-on because everyone can do this with the right information and tools. Without any guidance, it's too easy to avoid grief until the day that it slaps you upside down. But why is it so difficult to deal with directly?

Many of us were taught as children never to talk about it—to bury our feelings and pretend as if nothing had ever happened. More likely than not, we weren't given any tools to help us move forward after a loss. Our faith may tell us "everything happens for a reason" and that our loss is all a part of a "greater plan," but it doesn't necessarily ease the pain and sadness that the loss leaves behind.

I'm sure you've heard of the "five stages of grief": denial, anger, bargaining, depression, and acceptance. Unfortunately, grief doesn't unfold so neatly in stages. The reality is that your grief may, and probably will, feel different. Grief is unpredictable, uncertain, messy, and unsettling.

So what do we do then when we are stuck with complex feelings of guilt and anger?

Normally, we don't do anything. We let the grief simmer, hoping it doesn't boil over, but when it does—as is often the case—we break down.

But the very fact that you have picked up this book means that you are open to doing things differently.

You are choosing how you deal with grief and creating a space for hope.

You are taking your experiences with grief and using them to create a new life.

You are recognizing and accepting that you are no longer the person you were before your loss and allowing yourself to transform.

You are unabashedly allowing yourself to have feelings. Feel free to relive every detail of your loss, but know that you are not your feelings, and your thoughts are not facts. In time, these emotions and thoughts will diminish as you continue your commitment to heal.

You are stronger than you think you are. You'll walk through the fire and come out knowing you can handle doing it again and again, if necessary.

I did, and the first section of this book provides you with my own story battling the greatest grief of my life: losing my husband, Bill, to a suicide so violent it sent shockwaves through our community. Suicide is still a taboo subject that no one knows how to address, myself included at the time of Bill's death. Desperately hoping to find direction, I read dozens of books on grief. Instead, I continued feeling as if I were drowning. All I wanted was one book to get me moving in the right direction. It was too tempting to fall into the mindset that my life had ended because Bill was gone.

Ultimately, I figured out what worked for me. As I navigated a path through my grief, I kept notes about what helped me during my journey. I wanted to be prepared to help someone else when they needed it. Little did I know I would get into the grief recovery profession and write this book to help you or someone you know during the most heartbreaking of times.

What I Wish I'd Known is a self-care guide for grief. It will give you tools to put your grief behind you and live in the present. It's about learning to live with joy and pain, which can coexist in your heart. We are complex animals who are capable of running through a gamut of emotions in one day—and even one moment. You should never feel guilty for seeing the beauty around you, or feeling love, happiness, or even relief while suffering a loss.

In time, the sharp pain of grief can give way to a renewed sense of meaning and purpose. Your feelings of loss won't ever completely disappear, but they'll soften and the intense pangs of hurt or guilt will become less frequent. You'll be able to make commitments to the future. Know that your life can and will move forward.

I survived the traumatic loss of someone I loved very much, and I found the tools to not only thrive but also live a happy life again. I've taken a tragic event and learned the lessons that enabled me to become a better, more compassionate person. I came out of it with a newfound sense of what's important in life, and I learned that I have so much to give back to the world. Wrapping myself in a cloak of sorrow doesn't help me or anyone else—and certainly not the love that I lost. I hope I can help you realize the same.

Kristi Hugstad
October 2016

PART ONE

MY STORY

Chapter One

Life Is Beautiful

It was 2008, and my husband, Bill, was eagerly surfing the web for a vacation home for us in Baja, Mexico, just south of the border from our residence in Dana Point, California. We were toying with the idea of moving there. Life in our small beachside town was pretty wonderful, but we were drawn to the luxuriously sleepy pace and quaint culture of Baja. We felt it would fit us better in our later years. The American government had been warning citizens not to travel across the border because the drug cartels were out of control and the safety of tourists could not be guaranteed. Bill and I had traveled to Baja many times over the past few years. The people were friendly, and there were never any threats of violence in the places we visited. We were dedicated to making our shared dream of living in Mexico come true. Thinking about all the possibilities of this next chapter in our lives was exciting.

Little did I know that these possibilities would be entirely unfavorable, and life would never be the same again.

Bill and I had met five years earlier on a blind date set up by a mutual friend. We had a lot in common: We were in our mid-forties and worked in the fitness industry in the same beach city in Orange County. After the end of a ten-year relationship in Minneapolis, I had followed my sisters to Dana Point and established a peaceful, happy life on the coast for many years before I met Bill. Bill had also been living in Dana Point for just as long after the demise of a fourteen-year marriage in Texas, but he and I had never crossed paths. We'd both heard of one another but had never met.

I wasn't expecting our blind date to go well. I'd been through the ups and downs of dating for years. I was jaded and no longer excited about new dates. But when I first laid eyes on Bill, I couldn't help but be impressed. And when I found out he was funny and smart too, I was a goner.

Bill was one of those people you couldn't miss in a room. He was beautifully dressed, from his tailored Italian button-down shirt all the way down to his exquisitely crafted shoes. He had a massive, perfectly sculpted body, the result of years of weightlifting. His green eyes sparkled, and I liked his clean-cut look and shaved head. At six foot two, he was a great match for my five-foot-eleven height.

It turned out he was pretty smitten too. He had a thing for tall, blue-eyed blondes, and when he saw me, he immediately worried he wasn't tall enough. I had heels on, so he focused on straightening his posture all evening.

It was one of those perfect first dates that every person should get to have at least once in their life. The setting was beautiful: We sat in the lobby lounge of the Montage, arguably the most beautiful resort in Orange County. Our chemistry was instant and easy. We talked and laughed for hours as if we'd invented flirting. I didn't know what I wanted more: to hug him or hear what he was going to say next.

We moved from the lobby to the couch near the piano. He kept his arm on the back of the couch behind me. I thought that was very romantic. I liked the energy between us, and it seemed like he felt the same. He constantly leaned in to listen to my every word, and his twinkling eyes never lost contact with mine.

Everyone has a sense of humor, but humor itself is unique and subjective. I can be very dry and sarcastic, but Bill wasn't intimidated at all. He thought I was hilarious and witty, and seeing him not only handle my jokes but welcome them made me feel like I'd finally found someone with whom I could entirely be myself. It wasn't just a physical attraction. We knew this was something special.

Bill did not hesitate in expressing his admiration. He knew what he liked, and he was determined to make that clear. He called me the next day and every day from then on, several times a day. He began taking me to dinner at least four nights a week. In a very short time, we became inseparable. We married two years later.

Life together fell into place so easily from the beginning because we had so much in common. When we met, we each owned our own fitness business. I was the founder of the first spinning studio in Orange County, and Bill ran a successful weightlifting gym.

Eventually we merged our businesses and formed a gym together. We worked diligently to make it successful and complemented each other's strengths: I was the organizer and took care of the bills, office work, and all other mundane matters, while Bill was the marketer and visionary. At 240 pounds, he was all muscle—a walking advertisement for our gym with his honed physique. He was gregarious with an easy laugh and ready smile and lit up a room when he walked in.

I was thrilled to finally have someone with whom to share responsibilities and duties. The life of an entrepreneur can be taxing and lonely, so it was liberating to partner with Bill, who understood all the intricacies and headaches of the business. Our clients loved him, nicknaming him the "Gentle Giant." I was grateful to have found a man so perfectly aligned with everything I had ever hoped for in a husband, and he was happy to come home with me every night when we closed up our gym.

Our days started early, and our routine rarely varied. Bill would get up first, make himself breakfast, then bring me coffee and gently kiss me goodbye while I slowly roused myself from sleep. Later I would join him at the gym, where he was already training his first client of the day. I'd teach a spin class and Pilates in the back of the building while he stayed busy with clients in the front.

Yet we always found time to catch a minute here and there to say hello to each other and always smiled when we caught each other's eye. Our love and mutual admiration were evident to our clients, who enjoyed the ambiance created by a couple in love. Our business prospered.

We had purchased a condominium on the oceanfront that was just a few blocks from the gym. Every day at noon, Bill would head home to make us lunch. As a bodybuilder, he was an expert on nutrition and kept track of every calorie, ounce of protein, and gram of fat he consumed. He often ate a dozen eggs a day, yet had no issues with cholesterol.

I would come home to meet Bill for lunch. We squeezed in a little quality time every workday thanks to my oldest sibling, Debbie, who also covered for us when we weren't teaching or training. Because of her, we had flexibility for a business that was open long hours.

We'd savor our midday meal, then Bill would curl up with our cat, Smoke, and take a nap while I chugged away at my computer. Before heading back to the gym for our afternoon sessions, we'd spend an hour on the patio taking in the sunshine and enjoying the view.

I'd usually go back to the gym first, and I always relished the moment I'd see Bill riding his bike in later—a big, hulking guy in shorts and flip-flops dwarfing his bike and beaming at me ear-to-ear as he walked through the door. I just adored him.

Later I'd go home to start dinner while Bill stayed to work with evening clients. Eventually I'd hear his bike brakes—my cue to put the finishing touches on dinner. We'd talk about the day while I finished cooking. Then we'd eat and linger on the patio until we dragged ourselves into the kitchen to clean up.

We worked hard but our life was good, and we were happy. Usually we only took Sundays off, and they were always simple but special to us: We ran errands, did chores, went out for breakfast, and watched sports on TV. We didn't spend much time with friends—only my family occasionally. We were completely enamored with each other and wanted to spend time with only each other, so that's what we did. Every day.

Was it too good to be true? The question might have crossed your mind by now.

No relationship is perfect, but at the time I thought ours was pretty close to it. As they say, twenty-twenty is hindsight, and only now do I see how far we were from it. Bill's suicide didn't come out of nowhere. There were signs of mental instability all along, but I was naïve when it came to mental health. And just to throw another cliché at you, love is blind.

I grew up in Wanamingo, Minnesota (population 1,086), on a 240-acre farm with forty cows and 6,000 chickens. In just six years, my parents had five kids: Debbie, Viki, Scott, me, and Todd. We had free rein of the farm and spent countless days playing outdoors.

I couldn't have asked for a more stable childhood. I always imagined I'd live somewhere more eventful and exciting, but I knew I had a lot to be thankful for. We were pretty happy-go-lucky, and communication was never an issue—not even during our teen years. My parents were supportive and loving and urged us to explore our talents and desires.

Because of my upbringing, I assumed that people are generally stable if not also content. I knew depression existed, but it seemed irrelevant in my world. I'm sure I've had relatives, friends, and colleagues who have suffered from anxiety and depression—after all, it's been estimated that nearly 20 percent of Americans have experienced one or both—but they hid it so well I never witnessed it myself.

But even when I saw Bill experience these maladies, I didn't understand what was going on. Those years when we stayed secluded in our own cocoon built just for two? Occasionally, it did strike me that Bill was the one who insisted we be hermits. He didn't want to share me with anyone, and he complained often when I spent time with friends so I allowed those friendships to wither on the vine. However, he wasn't able to keep me from my mother and sisters. I told Bill that my family was off-limits, so, reluctantly, he allowed me to spend time with them.

If my family thought Bill was too possessive, they never said so. They loved me too much and were thrilled that I was finally in a relationship I'd always dreamed of. How many times have we all said, "Well if [s]he's happy, I'm happy?"

I also noticed that Bill became stressed easily. I'm the opposite—not much riles me. Priding myself on my ability to handle emergencies and solve challenging problems, I've always loved being a fixer. But the problem with being a fixer is that you're often the enabler. I didn't recognize until years after Bill's suicide that my role as the fixer enabled Bill to hide what was going on beneath his surface.

I first observed the extent of Bill's inability to handle stress when I discovered he hadn't paid his taxes in five years. We had been seeing each other seriously for more than a year when he confided to me that he feared getting his mail. He would only go to his mailbox once a week—

maybe even only every ten days. It turned out that he wasn't afraid of the mail. He was afraid of the IRS. Every time they sent a notice, he would go into denial mode and continue ignoring it.

I couldn't comprehend Bill's fear of the IRS, especially when I found out he had more than enough to pay what he owed. Moreover, he always paid his bills on time and was smart about keeping his overhead low. His credit was very good. Usually you fear the IRS because you don't have the money to pay your taxes and fines, but what was Bill so afraid of? He didn't know either.

Frustrated, I took all the receipts and paperwork he could find and visited his CPA. I walked him through the situation, brusquely asking what else he needed so that together we could get Bill caught up with the IRS. Wide-eyed, the CPA asked, "Why isn't Bill here? Where is Bill?"

It never occurred to me that Bill's absence was odd. All I cared about was fixing his tax problems so he wouldn't worry anymore. When you love someone, you want them to be happy. That's all I wanted for Bill.

Bill's inability to deal with anything deemed stressful showed his instability. I had missed that completely. Instead of acknowledging that he had a problem, I thought that taking care of whatever stressed him would help him. I didn't realize that Bill's helplessness showed he had deeper underlying issues, including having only the minimum coping skills required to thrive.

Year after year, problem after problem, we would discuss the issues but I would take care of them. It was our normal.

Bill was always loving and attentive, but sometimes he had a temper when he was anxious. He was never abusive, but he'd act out under stress. I hated seeing him feeling any combination of anger, anxiety, or stress, so eventually I became afraid of not immediately pouncing on anything that would disturb him. I told myself, "This is what marriage is—you love and you give and you keep moving forward." But I didn't comprehend that this wasn't "forward." In fact, we were running in emotional circles. We had unknowingly created a vicious cycle in which I enabled, and he avoided, his demons . . . that is, until the day he no longer could.

In 2009, Bill and I began heading south on the weekends to explore Rosarito, a West Coast town about an hour south of the US border. We had a blast delving into Rosarito's rich culture, which includes American settlers establishing working ranches in the early nineteenth century, an increase in tourism during Prohibition when Americans would travel to drink where it was legal, the Hollywood invasion that began in the 1950s, and much more.

By then, Bill and I were in our early fifties and were contemplating semiretiring in Rosarito. More and more baby boomers were flocking to the area, so new construction was flourishing. We decided to purchase a home there when we found a two-bedroom, two-bathroom condo on the eighth floor of a complex in Calafia. We were sold on its panoramic ocean view complete with amazing sunsets and dolphins and whales playing right outside our living room window.

We weren't ready to retire just yet, so we planned to set up a fitness business in Rosarito that we could manage part time. We arranged with the developer of our condo to split the costs of weight training equipment for the community gym in the downstairs lobby. Every other weekend we stayed in Rosarito, letting everyone know about our local training business and decorating and furnishing our new home. We also became regulars at a nearby fishing village where all the residents bought their fish.

With their boats pulled onto the sand, the fishermen sold their catch on the spot. Their prices varied widely and were always up for negotiation, but once they recognized me and Bill as regulars, we got the best rates. The merchants would skin and debone the fish, put our purchase in a plastic bag, and we would head home to prepare dinner. It doesn't get any fresher than that! We could see the village from our condo with binoculars, so we were always in the loop when the fishermen were on shore. There were no set market hours. You just watched them fish out at sea, then paid attention when they headed back to shore.

Those are just some of the simple pleasures I still miss to this day. When you lose someone, you don't necessarily yearn for the big, extravagant memories, such as your wedding day or that special vacation somewhere. Instead, you pine for the most modest privileges: going for long walks, napping, watching TV, or grilling and savoring a good piece of seafood together. But I'm glad to have had it than not.

In October 2011, we received an offer from an employee at our gym that was too good to pass up. He wanted to buy our gym, and he had a financial backer who could make that possible. The economy had slowed down significantly, and the Orange County real estate market had declined dramatically. We wanted to be debt-free, so we took a leap of faith, accepted the offer on our business, and sold our home. We would be putting a substantial amount of money in our savings, but we had worked hard and it was time to reap the rewards.

We searched for a rental home in Dana Point, but after having lived on the oceanfront for so long, nothing else seemed to compare. We discussed moving to Rosarito permanently: We weren't ready for semiretirement, but maybe we could grow our training business down there much more quickly if we were there full time we reasoned. We decided to sell all our belongings, say our goodbyes, and make the move. What could be more perfect than the life we had created there every other weekend?

And so we moved. In the beginning, it was blissful. Not having to make that Sunday drive back across the border and get up for work on Monday mornings was liberating. We started taking Spanish lessons with eight other Americans every Tuesday and Thursday afternoon. I studied and did the assignments diligently, but Bill used the excuse that he was never a very good student, so he didn't want to waste his time.

Actually, Bill had been an excellent student with an interest in engineering, even as a child. He dropped out of college his sophomore year to pursue bodybuilding. He spent the rest of his life regretting his decision and feeling self-conscious about his intelligence and capabilities. Even though he didn't study, he picked up Spanish quite easily and eventually helped me translate signs above the aisles of the local grocery stores.

I was so happy to see him engaging in our new foreign life, but this didn't last long. The Spanish classes stressed Bill out, and ever the enabler, I agreed to drop the classes. I just wanted him to adjust and enjoy, but if anything agitated him, I let him have his way.

Those first three months as permanent citizens of Rosarito were comprised of Spanish classes, grilling chicken or fish and whatever mystery vegetables the grocers suggested, lounging on our patio, which faced west (so every night we sat in awe of the most amazing sunset we'd ever seen), and working out on our brand new weight training equipment.

Chapter Two

Reality Sets In

No matter how much fun you have on vacation, most of us reach a point where we itch for home. Although Rosarito was home now, it still felt like a vacation—that is until three months had passed and Bill became bored with us being the only ones working out. Bill began to crave routine.

Every morning he rode down the elevator at seven thirty, keeping with his former schedule when he would train his first clients of the day at our old gym. He was struggling to keep up the same routine, and he was lonely working out with just me. There was no one around to give him input while he lifted. He observed that women were no longer hitting on him. I'd never realized how instrumental feedback was to his self-esteem.

We started exploring other gyms in the area, including a hole-in-the-wall run by a former Mr. Olympia. The two men sized each other up, and I could see that Bill was struggling with his identity: He had always been the best, the biggest, and the strongest, but here those things didn't matter so much to anyone except maybe Mr. Olympia.

If it was quiet in our gym before, it was now even quieter in our condo building. The Christmas season was over, the tourists had all returned home, and it was pretty much just the two of us. Whereas it had almost always been the two of us back in Dana Point, we'd been consumed by our business. In Rosarito, we had too much time on our hands and were joined at the hip. We went everywhere together: my hair appointments, gas station, taco shop, market, etc. When we'd first arrived, my car battery died and we'd never bothered to get it fixed. The novelty of Rosarito was wearing off. We'd had our fill of seafood. It was raining frequently, and the sun was setting before five. Perhaps most importantly, our training business had not taken off as we'd expected.

When we had first entertained the idea of moving to Baja, we were impressed by the booming retirement population. These people were wealthy enough to retire and young enough to want to stay fit. We hadn't considered that these particular retirees were on a fixed income: They could enjoy an affordable home and cheap cost of living, but they weren't about to indulge in any luxuries such as personal training.

Between us, we only had ten clients—not enough by the standards we were used to. I repeatedly advertised our business in the local paper but didn't get a single response. Things were looking grim.

Bill complained about everything. He started to skip his workouts. He followed me everywhere when I went out. When we were home, he sat and channel surfed. He never bothered to watch an entire program. He lost weight, and his clothes hung on him. He started to skip his sessions with his three steady clients, and I would apologize to them and make excuses for him.

Sometimes he'd pretend to jump off the balcony to get my attention. "Not funny!" I'd say, barely looking up. He wasn't feeling like his charismatic, energetic self, but I wasn't either. I truly did not know how deeply depressed he was. The only thing I knew was that our life in Rosarito was not turning out as expected.

Just like in the movies, there's always a turning point for everyone, and for us, it was the day Bill ran out of Halcion.

I look back now and still cringe at the memory. I never saw the signs. The world of prescription drugs was foreign to me, and I certainly didn't know anything about clinical depression or mental illnesses.

Halcion is the brand name for Triazolam, a sedative used to treat insomnia. It can cause paranoia or suicidal ideation and impair memory, judgment, and coordination. Bill used Halcion for seven years because he wrestled with falling asleep.

After Bill's prescription ran out in March 2012, he waited a few days before getting it refilled. Four days, if I remember correctly. I never asked why. I assumed he knew what was best because he was better versed in prescription medication than me.

Within those few days, panic set in. He experienced withdrawals, and he insisted we run to the pharmacy. We refilled the prescription, went home, and he tried to go to sleep.

But it was too late. The dosage no longer helped him sleep. He went through an entire bottle and still couldn't snooze.

Most of these drugs are available without prescriptions in Mexico, and sometimes you don't know what you're actually getting. Whether Bill had too many days away from Halcion or he'd received a bad knockoff, he returned to the pharmacy and requested a stronger dosage. It didn't work either.

His insomnia worsened. One early morning around two, Bill got out of bed and began pacing frantically around our home.

"Bill," I said, rousing myself from sleep, "what can I do to help?"

"I don't know," he replied. "I've never felt so anxious in my life. Kristi, it's like my skin is crawling."

He began mumbling to himself, raising his arm in the air, and snapping his fingers. I had never seen him like this. He did this the entire night. Helpless, I stayed up with him for support.

I called our Rosarito real estate agent and asked for the name of a good psychologist, whom he himself had seen. I immediately made an appointment with Lily, and she worked with Bill on the art of deep breathing. Bill learned to calm himself and even occasionally put himself back to sleep, but it wasn't enough. On his next appointment, his anxiety was so out of control that Lily conceded Bill was beyond her help. She referred us to another doctor.

I pleaded with the new doctor to prescribe anything for Bill to help him sleep. He was turning into someone I didn't recognize. Reluctantly, the doctor gave Bill a prescription for Valium, but even this did not help Bill sleep or relax. Apparently, he had become immune to any calming substances.

To make matters worse, Bill's dad was coming to visit us from Texas.

Bill was born and raised an only child in Pasadena, a suburb of Houston. His father, Bill Sr., was a successful CEO in the oil industry, and his mother was a homemaker and socialite. Together, they enjoyed a glamorous life of traveling and hobnobbing with others in their successful circle.

Their life had been full and busy to the degree that Bill was not always their priority. At just twelve years old, Bill was sometimes left home alone overnight. At an even younger age when his parents were attending parties, he was often worried and scared and waited up till they came home in the wee hours of the morning.

He learned to keep himself entertained and spent many nights making toys with matchsticks, which also shows you what a good child Bill was. Not once did he think of setting anything on fire; he just wanted to stay busy until his parents came home.

I never really minded how much Bill clung to me because I sympathized for the child within. He had never dealt with his fear of abandonment. His parents hadn't made him a priority, so I made him mine.

Bill was an amazing athlete in high school. Having felt neglected for most of his life, he reveled in the attention he received as an athletic wonder in football, basketball, and baseball.

After his college roommate introduced him to bodybuilding, he left college at nineteen and entered the competitive world of the sport. To support himself, he worked for a telephone company and created architectural drawings. He earned a good living but always regretted that he hadn't finished his engineering degree. For the rest of his life, he never let himself forget that he was a college dropout.

Bill appeared to be close to his parents and talked to his father on the phone often, but it was superficial. Bill Sr. was retired and occasionally visited us. Bill's mother, Bess, rarely visited; she didn't like to fly. At that point, she hadn't seen her son in five years. We couldn't make it to Texas ourselves. We'd always been so busy with the gym that we couldn't afford to be away longer than a weekend.

I wasn't sure how much Bill Sr. had picked up on Bill's condition from their conversations. I worried whether his trip would make Bill more anxious or actually help him. During his father's four-day stay, Bill was in a constant state of panic and continually apologized to his dad for his nonstop pacing and agitated behavior.

Either Bill Sr. didn't notice or chose to ignore it because he acted as if his son's behavior was nothing out of the ordinary. He seemed to love Rosarito even though it rained relentlessly during his visit.

But on his last night, Bill Sr. shared with us some personal information that even Bill had never known. He said that both of Bill's grandmothers had attempted suicide and suffered from severe depression. His maternal grandmother had even been placed in an institution and received electric shock treatment.

Then he admitted that he too had been an insomniac for more than forty years. Tears filled his eyes, and he struggled to hold them back. It hit me then that Bill Sr. did see that something was wrong with his son.

I kept glancing at Bill, who was taking all the revelations in stride. I looked at Bill Sr., unsure whether he'd traveled here because he'd sensed that something was wrong. I still don't know if Bill realized that his father might have been insinuating that his problems could be attributed to an inherited condition.

And as for me? I wasn't sure what to think, but I knew I didn't like it. I didn't know then that there are genetic links to suicidal behavior. Nor did I understand the significance that Bill had mental illness on both sides of his family.

Sensing his son was stressed, Bill Sr. suggested we return to California so Bill could work as a personal trainer for senior citizens. "Or if you move to Texas," he offered, "I can introduce you to oilmen who need inspectors for their offshore rigs."

Bill looked away, trying hard not to show his agitation. For Bill, Texas symbolized a time in his life when he was struggling. Going back would mean failing.

The whole visit exhausted all of us. We drove Bill Sr. across the border to San Diego International Airport and said our goodbyes. When he hugged Bill, I noticed tears in his eyes again.

Tears were rare for this old-school, rugged man who had always told his only child, "Always take care of number one: you!"

The minute Bill Sr. was out of our sight, Bill turned to me and said, "There is no way I'm ever moving to Texas."

Chapter Three

It Gets Worse

After Bill's father left, the situation got worse. Bill's next bout of anxiety attacks and insomnia lasted four days straight. He couldn't stop pacing around the condo. Panicked, he yelled constantly, "GET ME OUT OF HERE! GET ME OUT OF THIS TRAVERTINE BOX! I HATE IT! I'M FREEZING! WHY DID WE MOVE HERE?"

He let loose with a series of guttural screams that I can still hear in my head. If we'd had neighbors, I'm sure they would have thought I was torturing him.

I didn't know what to do. I was in a foreign country where I wasn't fluent in the language and didn't know where to turn for help. I sat at the computer sobbing while I researched various hospitals in Rosarito and San Diego. Bill was completely out of his mind, and I couldn't reason with him.

He refused to leave the condo. He didn't seem to notice whether I was present. He was alone in his own world.

I hadn't slept in four days either, so when my sister Viki called, I broke down. I had been trying to handle everything on my own and hadn't confided to any of my friends or family back in the States what had been going on with Bill. He had begged me not to involve anyone. I agreed because I thought he'd be embarrassed once he got better.

I really did believe that Bill would get better. I thought it was a phase and that if he just got enough sleep, everything would be okay. I didn't know there were dots all along that I could have connected: the inability to handle stress, fear of abandonment, inflexibility outside of his comfort zone, and dependence on prescription drugs and steroids. The latter he'd used a great deal in his bodybuilding days, but did his minimal use now still have an effect?

Viki immediately offered her support and arrived the next day with our mother, other sister Debbie, and Debbie's daughter, Tess. We took Bill to the main hospital, where she explained to the doctor in her fluent Spanish that he was extremely sick and suicidal. She asked if they had an inpatient facility where Bill could be admitted. They did not. Instead, they gave him an injection that put him out for eight hours, but when he woke up and was released, the nightmare started all over again.

We had only been living in Rosarito for six months. It was time to wave the white flag. This adventure of living in a foreign country wasn't working for us.

I started asking for help. A couple of neighbors in our condo building had an empty home back in Orange County and offered to rent it to us until I got help for Bill and got us back on our feet. It was a huge relief. I started making plans and packing. I left nothing to Bill so that he wouldn't have to deal with any additional stress.

But two days before the move, our neighbors rescinded their offer. They weren't comfortable with Bill living in their home in his unstable condition.

I pleaded and offered six months' rent up front, but they made it clear that there was no room for further discussion. The offer was off the table.

I was afraid the news would be more than Bill could handle. Any little thing would send him into a rage. He complained endlessly about what a mistake it had been to buy our condo in Rosarito. How quickly he had forgotten that it had once been his dream!

Debbie found an apartment for rent in the same area where we'd lived and made arrangements for us to see it. I packed our belongings in plastic bags and had someone jumpstart my car. We drove both cars across the border back to the same town we had just left six months earlier when we were full of optimism and adventure.

The new apartment was small and dark, but I just needed a place for us to get settled so I could get Bill help. We didn't have any furniture, which further aggravated Bill. Viki took us shopping for essentials. Soon we had a bed and a few other pieces of furniture to fill the void.

The next day I took Bill to a walk-in clinic. After a doctor examined him, she admitted that she wasn't equipped to handle Bill in his current mental health state. She recommended two psychiatrists. Immediately, I made an appointment with the one closest to us.

At our appointment, the psychiatrist demanded cash. He was in a small office without a receptionist and didn't have a single piece of artwork or a framed diploma on the wall. I was worried.

He listened to Bill, and then prescribed him a smorgasbord of medications. Bill would ask about a certain drug, and the doctor would say, "Sure!" and write that one down too.

I wasn't convinced that Bill's problems were going to be solved this way, so I made an appointment with the other psychiatrist. It was the same thing, but I didn't know what other choice we had. Bill continued seeing him and left with a new prescription after every visit.

Even though more prescriptions were not the answer, Bill seemed calmer, and this gave me more time to think. I knew he was anxious about money, dreary living arrangements, and getting work, but he was also becoming more sensitive about even inconsequential things.

"The neighbors are too noisy."

"There's not enough water pressure."

"We're having this for dinner again?"

"The bathroom's too small and the showerhead's too low."

"It's too hot . . . Now it's too cold."

I still held hope that I could fix everything. If I could just find us a better place to live and rebuild my client base in Dana Point, I could alleviate some of the pressure Bill felt. I was sure this would give us a better shot at getting our old life back. These things all seemed very doable, and I felt like I was starting to get a handle on it all.

Chapter Four

Two Steps Back

I woke to hear Bill tinkering in the kitchen. *Oh good, he's making coffee,* I thought. Any semblance of a normal routine gave me hope. We'd only been back for a few weeks in Dana Point, and I hoped that our time in our old stomping grounds would make Bill feel more grounded.

I heard the door to the bathroom close, and I got up and went to the kitchen. There on the table, I found a note. It read:

Baby, you need to move on with your life and find somebody better.
I can't do this anymore.
Love, Bill

It read like a suicide note. I ran into the bathroom and found Bill taking a shower.

"What did you take?" I screamed.

"Twenty Ambien and half a bottle of Nyquil," he said calmly.

He seemed quite coherent. He was a large man, but surely if he had taken that much Ambien and Nyquil, wouldn't he have been sluggish? It seemed more like a cry for attention and help.

Immediately I called Debbie, who rushed over. Together she and I spent two hours coaxing Bill to get into her car to go to the hospital. He had moved out of the bathroom to our bedroom, where he sat silently on the edge of the bed with his head in his hands. Debbie and I exchanged glances every few minutes. She was checking in to see how I was dealing with this, and I was thanking her with my eyes for being here for me and Bill.

This was a living hell. What else could I do for this man whom I loved so deeply?

To my relief, eventually Bill agreed to get into the passenger seat of Debbie's car, and the three of us drove to the nearest hospital in deafening silence.

In the emergency room, Bill was placed on a "5150"—an involuntary psychiatric hold, where he would remain for seventy-two hours on suicide watch. They took away his shoestrings, belt, and anything else that he could use to harm himself. He changed into a gown and lay on the hospital bed. They sedated him, took blood for testing, and then left us alone. However, he was within sight of a nurse at all times.

A few hours later, a nurse informed me that since Bill didn't have health insurance, he would be transported to a county facility. She told me to go home because visiting hours were over and the medics were going to transport Bill to the new location.

I watched in horror as they tried to lift him onto the gurney. He didn't know what was going on. Confused and scared, he tried to resist.

Once they got him under control, they strapped his wrists and ankles while he screamed my name and demanded answers. "Where are they taking me? What's going on?"

I tried to comfort him, assuring him that they were taking him to a facility that was better equipped to help him. I had no idea what a huge lie that would turn out to be.

As the red lights of the ambulance began to spin as it headed down the driveway, I sat on the curb and sobbed. I was completely spent.

By the time I returned home, I received a call from Bill at the county hospital. He told me one of his old gym members had recognized him upon admittance, and asked him what he was doing there—to which Bill replied, "It's all a big mistake!" He continued lying, explaining that he had simply taken some pills to sleep and someone had thought he'd taken too many and was trying to commit suicide.

After hanging up, I immediately called the hospital and asked to speak to the doctor who was treating Bill. The nurse on the other end of the line said he would not be seeing a doctor that night. I tried to explain to her that he needed proper treatment, that he was depressed and suicidal. She assured me she would do her best.

The next morning Bill called me and told me to come get him. Good news! The doctor had just met with him and released him.

I was flabbergasted. There would be no help, no treatment, nothing. I couldn't think beyond the next second. At that very moment, all I could do was focus on breathing.

I agonized during the entire drive to the county hospital. How was Bill going to react to having been coerced into going to the hospital and strapped down and taken to the county facility where all the homeless and drunk people are taken?

When they finally brought him out, he just hugged me. I asked him if he was okay, and he said yes. When we got home, he picked up Smoke and started to channel surf. I was sad watching him do this for what seemed like the thousandth time these last few months. It was how he self-soothed; it was his safety zone.

Bill continued getting even more vocal about how much he hated the apartment. “I’d give anything to get out of this toxic dump,” he said.

I had been looking for a better housing situation and had located a nice oceanfront duplex near our old home. It was beautiful. The view was even better. He would be thrilled.

When he saw it, he scowled. “It faces too far to the east, and we’re not going to get any sun after one,” he complained.

In that moment I felt defeated, but I refused to lose what hope I had left.

Chapter Five

The Descent

One Sunday morning near the end of May, Bill got out of bed, grabbed his keys, and left without saying a word. This wasn't like him.

These days, he rarely left the apartment. Apart from training his clients—we were working at a local gym—he avoided people. I began rebuilding my clientele and maintained a following in my Pilates classes. Bill had three new training clients—the maximum number he was interested in pursuing. He spent most of his day watching TV at home. I began staying at work longer and taking more time to run errands or go for runs just to give myself some quiet time.

Moreover, Bill had always been the kind of partner who kept me posted on his whereabouts and when he'd be back. This particular morning, I noticed he'd left his cell phone behind, which seemed more intentional than forgetful. Apprehension flooded me. I steadied my breath. I reminded myself that he seemed calmer lately and that I was worrying for nothing.

We were planning to go to Debbie's house for Viki's birthday dinner in the late afternoon, but eight hours later, he still wasn't home. Bill Sr. called to check in, and I told him that Bill had left and I was scared.

If Bill Sr. was aware of how troubled his son was, he didn't say it, but he did feel it necessary to immediately hang up with me and call the police to file a missing person's report. The police showed up at our apartment to get a description of Bill and any other details I might know.

After they left, I sat crying at the kitchen table. I felt powerless and vulnerable, two things a fixer despises feeling. Bill Sr. called repeatedly to find out whether I had any new information. My family waited by the phone for news. It was pure emotional chaos.

Suddenly, Bill walked in the front door calm as can be. He didn't even notice my hysterical state. The top of his head was burned so badly I could see blisters.

I asked what he had been doing, and he replied, "Walking next to the train tracks."

The tracks were about three miles from our apartment. He had gone there and just walked back and forth, he said.

He apologized for not calling. He'd simply lost track of time and then realized he'd left his cell phone at home. Then he walked into the bedroom and lay down with Smoke, turned on the TV, and started to channel surf.

I tried to draw on whatever optimism I had left. Even though he had complained about the gorgeous oceanfront duplex I'd recently shown him, I'd signed the lease and forged his name. Regardless of the eastern-facing view, it would be an improvement over the horrible little apartment we were currently in. It cost several thousand dollars to break the lease, but I'd thought it was worth it. I didn't want Bill's fragile state to worsen, so I furtively applied for a credit card to pay off our lease. Writing a check would have immediately flagged Bill when he checked our bank account.

Bill was swimming deep in pessimism. Once sunny and positive, he couldn't even try to see the upside to a situation anymore. He was also becoming more paranoid about my behavior and came up with the outlandish notion that I had a boyfriend on the side. He started going through my personal things looking for evidence of infidelity. Eventually he found the secret credit card and was sure it was for an apartment that I had with this imaginary lover.

He was also becoming more obsessed with suicide and death. He would take a kitchen knife and pretend to stab himself in the stomach. Sometimes he climbed over the safety railings along the nearby cliffs and pretended he was going to jump. He became obsessed with a young gym member of ours who had committed suicide near our home. His fixation became so common I no longer took his threats seriously. I was sure he wouldn't be so cruel as to inflict that kind of pain on his parents or me.

There would be one problem with the move: Pets were not allowed in our new duplex. I was so sure this new home would fix Bill's problems that I gave up Smoke, whom I'd loved for sixteen years. My friend's mother took her. I had reasoned that Smoke was better off in a home with less stress.

On moving day, I told Bill to leave everything to me. I promised it would cost nothing. He left me and Debbie in peace. When he came home that evening, everything was unpacked and put away neatly.

But that first night we heard a dog howling upstairs. The next day I called the landlord to let him know I knew our neighbor had a dog. I asked if I could bring Smoke, who was quiet and very old. He agreed, and I eagerly left to retrieve her.

Only then did I realize it had been two days since we'd moved, and even though Bill cuddled with Smoke every evening, he hadn't noticed she'd been missing.

Shortly after our move, Bill's parents decided to visit us for a week. It was July, and they didn't want to miss the beautiful summer weather. Initially, they asked to stay with us, but the duplex only had one bedroom, and we didn't want them to witness Bill's state of mind. Again, I was trying to protect my husband from the potential embarrassment of his mental condition.

We were relieved when they reserved a room at the Marina Inn in the Dana Point Harbor. It was conveniently located to many shops and restaurants, so they could spend most of the day—if they had to—entertaining themselves. Bill played host as well as he could. It was imperative that his parents have a wonderful trip since his mother rarely visited.

The second night of their visit, we took them to dinner at Olemendi's in Dana Point because Bess, Bill's mom, loved Mexican food. It was directly across from the train tracks that Bill had walked along just a couple of months before. We enjoyed our dinner as we watched the train ride by.

The next evening, we barbecued at our new home. We wanted to share the view with Bill's parents. Bill was extremely quiet during dinner so I tried to make up for his silence by making small talk with his father. Bill Sr. enjoyed reminiscing about his upbringing and regaling us with stories about his career, so conversation flowed easily. Bill's parents didn't seem to notice Bill's reticence.

As the evening wound down, I felt the need to tell Bill Sr. and Bess about their son's depression. I explained that I was desperately trying to find him the help he needed. They refused to participate; instead, Bill Sr. changed the subject and started telling another one of his stories.

My eyes stung with tears. I wanted their help, and they were making it very clear that I wasn't going to get it. I broke down, and Bill quickly took his parents back down to the harbor.

Two nights later, we held another dinner for Bill's parents but this time I also invited my mother and sisters. I hoped that with my family there, Bill Sr. and Bess would no longer avoid the issue. But the evening was a repeat of the previous dinner. Bill Sr. monopolized the conversation while my family and I exchanged bewildered looks.

The next morning, my mom and sisters called me, offering to come back again and stage an intervention with Bill's parents. I was eager to try anything. I was at my wit's end.

But when Bill invited his parents to come to our home, Bess said she preferred not to. "Kristi is far too emotional, and it makes me uncomfortable," she explained to her son. That evening, Bill and I had dinner alone in silence while his parents dined on the harbor.

When it was time to return home to Texas, Bill Sr. and Bess visited us for a few hours. Bill told them that my family disliked their refusal to acknowledge he needed help. My family had wanted them to understand how critical it was to figure out a treatment plan for Bill.

Bill's parents weren't flustered at all. They told him everything would work out. Even knowing their own history of mental illness on both sides of the family, they remained in denial.

"You just need to be more patient," they told us.

It was the last time Bill and Bess would ever see their only child.

Chapter Six

Losing Touch

You tend to remember the individual days that lead up to the one that changes everything forever. For me, October 8 will always be the day Bill discovered my nervous picking habit and his diminishing triceps. I relive that day and every day until October 12 because they are still so vivid. I try to take each memory apart, no matter how inconsequential, as if I were a literature scholar. I analyze every word, phrase, and interaction between the characters that were Bill and I.

It was October 8 when Bill pulled back the sheets covering me and gasped at the sight of blood all over them. I had developed a nervous habit of scratching my right arm until it bled. Night after night, our sheets had been covered with blood. He hadn't noticed until now.

As he reached out to look at my arm, he noticed his own arm and became distracted by it. "Look at my triceps," he said. "They're getting so small."

He turned and walked away to look at his arms in the mirror, forgetting about the blood all over our bed. He had become completely self-consumed.

We had only been living in the new duplex for a few months. Things weren't improving. I was exhausted from trying to defend myself from his ridiculous accusations, trying to keep him calm and make him happy, trying to get him help from doctors, counselors, psychologists, and anyone else who would listen.

I was going to such extremes that when Bill complained that the railings of our patio were too high—thus preventing him from seeing the view from our deck chairs—I hired a handyman to build taller lounge chairs so he could be completely immersed in the view. I was officially tired of being the fixer.

The following night, October 9, Bill started an argument over a pair of jeans he thought were missing from my closet. He was sure I had taken them to the imaginary apartment I shared with my supposed boyfriend.

He followed me into the bathroom, demanding to know the name of my new boyfriend. It struck me that his paranoia was very serious now. As I was leaving the bathroom, Bill stretched out his arm and blocked the doorway so I couldn't leave. I begged him to let me out; he refused.

I tried to pull his arm away from the doorway, and when I could not, I burst into tears. For the first time in our relationship, I was afraid of him.

I told Bill I was going to Debbie's for the night. "You're scaring me," I sobbed.

He angrily demanded a name. "Don't go there," I said, but he was adamant in his request. Panicked, I began making up names. The look on his face didn't change. He knew I was lying to appease him. I pushed again at his arm, and finally he let me go.

"I hate myself so much," he said tearfully. "How could you love me?"

I was flabbergasted. Was he looking for a reason to turn on me, or turn me away from him?

I grabbed my workout bag and threw a couple of items in it. *I need space*, I thought. I needed one evening away, and he needed one evening alone to think.

As I walked out the door, Bill asked if I was going to the store first because there wasn't any food in the house. He was more concerned about dinner right now!

"Incredible!" I exclaimed as I got in my car, shaking. As I headed toward Debbie's house, my phone kept buzzing with calls from Bill. Livid, I ignored them.

Halfway to Debbie's, the check engine light came on, but I continued to drive. Then my car stalled and died in the middle of traffic. I couldn't get it restarted. Frantic, I called Debbie. She told me to stay put and sent a tow truck for me.

Only then did I return Bill's calls. He said he would come get me. "It's fine," I told him. "The tow truck is coming. Everything's under control."

The tow truck arrived and towed me to the nearest station. Bill stopped calling. Debbie picked me up and took me back to her house.

The next morning I borrowed her car and drove by the duplex to grab my running shoes for a private training session. I couldn't handle another confrontation, so I waited around the corner, stealthily watching for Bill to leave.

I sat there with my heart pounding. I couldn't believe this was what my life had become. I never thought I'd be afraid of my own husband. I never imagined that Bill could be the kind of man to hurt anyone, and yet he had become a stranger over the past ten months. I didn't really know him anymore. Maybe I was in much more denial than I could even bring myself to admit. There were times when he would pretend to jump off the balcony, reaching out his hand to me, inviting me to join him. Was I overreacting to his drama or was he seriously as disturbed as he seemed?

After half an hour, Bill still hadn't left for work. I didn't want to be late meeting my client, so I left and met her at the harbor.

Bill could see us from the balcony of the duplex, and immediately got in his car and headed to the harbor. By the time he arrived there, however, I was already in my sister's car and drove right past him. He didn't recognize me in her car. I could see him scanning the sidewalks left and right for me.

He looked anxious and frantic. He was driving but I imagined that if he had been on foot, he would have looked like a caged animal pacing back and forth.

I picked up my shoes from our house and went into the gym to teach classes the rest of the day. I knew I wouldn't run into him there because he didn't have any other clients that day. But every so often I would look up and catch a glimpse of his car, slowly driving by the parking lot looking for me or my car.

I was relieved when hours had passed and I realized he had given up his search for me. I could focus on work now and think about what to do with Bill later. I wanted him to settle down and think. Even then, I still believed he could be capable of thinking logically and making rational decisions. I believed if he could only think straight, he'd conclude that together we could fix this.

When I left the gym late that afternoon, I noticed a big commotion just a little ways away—somewhere past the harbor, near the railroad tracks. Sirens and emergency vehicles stopped traffic as I headed toward my sister's house.

I spent another night there and kept my phone turned off. I wasn't ready to hear from Bill. I wanted him to spend time reflecting and see that I was serious about not putting up with his behavior any longer. This was the longest we had ever been apart since we had started dating.

Debbie and I didn't talk much about Bill. We hadn't had any real quality time alone together in the last year aside from her helping me with the apartment moves and with Bill. We wanted to enjoy our time together and give me a brief respite from Bill. We agreed that two nights at her house were enough to send him the right message.

I had an appointment to train a client early the next morning back on the harbor, but when I got there, it started to rain. I checked my cell phone. Sure enough, she had cancelled. That's when I discovered eight voicemails from my in-laws (but none from Bill). I assumed they must have spoken to him and were now calling to check on me. Silently I rehearsed what to tell them to put their minds at ease: We were just on a temporary break and they needn't worry—we would be able to work things out. I dialed their number, and Bess answered immediately.

Chapter Seven

The Aftermath

Bess could barely speak. Her voice was shaking. "There's been an accident," she said. "A train hit Bill."

"An accident? Was he in his car? Was he on foot?" I asked, confused. Bill must have been in his car and the car protected him from injury or death. *Yes, this had to be what happened*, I thought.

Bess told me to find Bill Sr. at the Marina Inn. I was confused. He was here? How could he have gotten here so quickly from Houston?

The rain poured that day—a rarity in southern California. I was drowning in emotions. I couldn't embrace the reality of what I'd just been told. I began to slump over the steering wheel and gasp.

Deep in my heart I knew this wasn't an accident. Bill was dead. If I went to his father's motel, I would learn the truth. I didn't want to know.

Briefly I contemplated driving into a light pole. I wanted to escape what was about to unfold.

The morning before, Bill had called his parents. "My head is scrambled," he'd said.

His father had quickly put together a plan: He would fly to California, bring Bill home to Texas, help him get a new job, and get him to a mental health clinic. He'd booked the first flight available to San Diego and had estimated he would arrive just after five p.m. after taking the train from San Diego to San Juan Capistrano. That's where Bill typically picked him up.

At two thirty when his plane arrived, Bill Sr. had called his son to check in. Bill assured his father that he was fine. And so Bill Sr. boarded the train and settled into his seat, ready to help his son.

But at some point, Bill Sr. felt the train come to an unplanned stop. He called Bill to tell him about the delay, but Bill didn't respond. He overheard a passenger across the aisle talking on the phone: "There's been a death on the tracks."

Not for one second did Bill Sr. think his son had stepped in front of his train.

They were delayed for several hours. After Bill Sr. finally arrived at the San Juan Capistrano station, he looked for his son's car but without luck. He assumed Bill had grown tired of waiting and had returned home. He continued calling Bill and finally flagged a taxi and went to the Marina Inn.

Bill must have taken a sleeping pill, so he's out cold now, he thought.

It wasn't until the next morning that he put two and two together.

He called the coroner.

I ran through the Marina Inn's front doors soaked from the rain, screaming for the desk clerk to give me Bill Sr.'s room number. "Ma'am, that's not information I can give you," he said gently.

I exploded, "My husband killed himself."

Stunned, the clerk immediately said, "301," and I ran into the elevator.

Bill Sr.'s door was cracked open. I called out his name, and he looked out. There stood an eighty-year-old, gray-skinned man hunched over. His face was expressionless. He didn't speak. I hugged him, but he responded as if I were a stranger.

"The coroner just called," he finally said. "They confirmed that the man who ran in front of the train I was on was Bill."

I felt as if the walls around me were collapsing. I had to get out. I ran to the car and called my mother. It was eight thirty in the morning on October 11. As usual, she greeted me pleasantly and asked how I was.

"Mom," I sobbed, "Bill killed himself. He ran in front of a train."

As the rain continued to pour, I sat in the car crying. My mother and Debbie suddenly appeared at my window. They opened the car door, and my eighty-year-old mother mustered the strength to hold me up and rock me.

We went into the motel to find Bill Sr. and learned that he had woken up that morning completely unaware that his son had died. It wasn't until he'd gone downstairs for breakfast that he overheard guests in the breakfast room talking about a local man who had been hit by the train the night before. It was then that he realized that man was his son.

Remember when Bill disappeared and came home eight hours later with a sunburnt head? He'd walked up and down the train tracks, he explained. But it wasn't a neurotic pacing after all. He had been rehearsing his death, and for whatever reason that Sunday, he'd decided it wasn't the right time.

After Bill died, I went through the search history on his computer. I found searches for "how to make cyanide" and "train schedule" multiple times on different days. He had been thinking about suicide for a long time.

I later learned that people often not only rehearse their acts of suicide but also act out physically how they want their suicides to play out. Bill had planned the exact location as well as where he would hide and wait for the train.

I've spent countless hours examining every angle of every moment I've shared with Bill and all the days that led up to his suicide. It was my own way of torturing and punishing myself for failing to save Bill from his demons.

In the immediate years after Bill's death, I decided the root of his illness was long-term use of anabolic steroids and prescription drugs. But just like any situation, time changes your perspective. I've learned that when it comes to death, there isn't always one simple story. There are many things that had to have happened that all led up to one ending. It's never black and white.

Sure, Bill's illness could have had a great deal to do with steroids and drugs, but it could also have been hereditary, a chemical imbalance, or maybe even inflamed by his upbringing. Ultimately, it was a combination of many things—all leading to a perfect storm.

For most of us with a healthy mind, our greatest fear is death. But for Bill—or a mentally ill or clinically depressed person—his greatest fear was life.

Bill did not leave a note. Instead, he left us with a lot of questions that I'll never have answers to. I can't be sure that Bill knew his father was on that very train. Logic suggests that he must have known, because he knew what time to pick up Bill Sr. The only thing I'm certain of is that he was determined never to step foot back in Texas—certainly not for the reasons that his parents wanted him to return. Maybe he didn't feel strong enough anymore to fight for himself or argue with Bill Sr. Maybe he was mad at his dad. Maybe he was scared of his dad. Maybe he loved his dad too much to let him see him this way.

The toxicology report was clean. Did it mean he was of sound mind when he stood in front of the train? Was he so mad at me that he didn't take the time to write me a note? What were his last thoughts of me and his parents?

Were his accusations of infidelity his way of turning us against each other or even seeking reason or permission to go ahead with his suicide plan? It's hard to understand that someone could be so mentally ill or clinically depressed that he could create such an outrageous scenario. Believing that I would ever be unfaithful was really about him. He was so full of low self-esteem and self-hatred that he couldn't fathom that anyone, especially his own wife, would want to remain by his side.

Besieged by confusion, my life suddenly became full of what-ifs and maybes, but I had no choice but to carry on with the motions.

I did what was expected of me. I returned the call to the coroner; he offered condolences and confirmed that it was indeed Bill who had been hit by the train. I went to the funeral home with my mother, Bill Sr., Debbie, and Viki. They picked out a moderately priced urn. I was too numb to care.

The funeral director asked me if I wanted to identify the body, which led me to believe it was still intact. *Maybe he didn't die as horrifically as I keep imagining*, I reasoned.

My family firmly shook their heads. I went along with whatever they suggested. I'm glad I listened: Later I learned that very little left of his body was left. I don't know if I would have been able to get over seeing Bill that way for the last time.

At first I didn't want to hold a memorial service because it would be too painful, but I realized so many people in the community needed closure. Surprisingly, though, some of Bill's longtime clients and gym members didn't come or ever acknowledge what happened. Not only did they not attend his service, they didn't send flowers or cards. They didn't even leave a voicemail.

It was my first taste of the taboo: Suicide is just too scary for some people.

Bill Sr. stayed for the memorial, but Bess chose to stay home. She said it was just too hard for her and she didn't like to fly.

Bill's parents requested that the ashes be flown to them in Houston. Bill Sr. asked me to arrange for the ashes to arrive on a Thursday, when Bess had her weekly hair appointment. I couldn't control when the package arrived. Unfortunately Bess wound up receiving her son's remains.

In the weeks that followed, I avoided going to places where I might run into people we had known. There were long-time clients who hadn't reached out to me, and if I did see them, they would awkwardly attempt to hug me. Often they'd tell me how they had just been thinking of Bill and wished I knew how much they cared.

I'd nod politely, but inside I was crushed. I wanted to cry, "How do I know you care if you don't let me know? Do I have to run into you so you can tell me?"

The first week after Bill's suicide, my mom and sisters took turns staying with me overnight, but eventually they had to return to their lives, and I had to start living mine—alone. I was terrified to go to sleep because I dreaded waking up every morning and realizing that it wasn't a bad dream after all.

I returned to my job, where I worked in a small space with the windows facing out into a large gym. I watched hundreds of gym members awkwardly turn away when they saw me. They didn't know what to say to me, so they said nothing. That's when I learned an important rule of comforting the bereaved:

> *Saying nothing, or not acknowledging someone in pain who is a mourning a tragic loss, is the worst thing someone can do. Just showing up is what's important.*

At first my grief felt like someone had kicked me hard in the stomach and left their boot firmly implanted. I couldn't stand up straight. I couldn't eat. I was afraid of sleep. It felt like I'd feel this way forever, and there wasn't a thing I could do to make the pain and suffering stop.

I searched the Internet for every book I could find on grief, mourning, depression, suicide, steroid and drug withdrawal, anxiety, afterlife . . . all in hopes of finding answers.

I questioned God. *What was the purpose of this journey with Bill?* I asked constantly. *I'm a good person. I treat people well. I have integrity and morals. Why me?*

I was so immersed in my search for logic and explanation that I didn't realize other people were moving on with their lives. Anger and resentment don't even touch upon what I felt whenever people complained about the weather. "How can you complain about cloudy skies when my husband is dead?" I literally bit my tongue from asking.

I reached out to Bill's parents often. Bess never took my calls. Bill Sr. made small talk—mainly about his goat ranch, which he had purchased upon retirement. It kept him busy, and he welcomed the distraction. Neither parent took any action to address the pain caused by the loss of their son. These days they don't take or return my calls anymore. Periodically I call and leave voicemails updating them on what's new in my life, but I stopped expecting a response years ago. I call anyway because they are as tied to Bill as I am.

Chapter Eight

A New Journey

At some point that only you will know you have reached, you will have to make a choice: Strive for some semblance of happiness or wallow in deep sadness. Bill died in October 2012, and by December, I had speaking engagements at a local college and a number of high schools. I talked about suicide, depression, and anxiety. I talked about looking at the person next to you and asking the simplest of questions: "Are you okay?"

Before Bill's death, I didn't have much of a plan, purpose, or desire to make a difference. I was happy skating through life. Business was good, clients were happy, family was healthy. But with Bill gone, I was faced with remnants of a broken heart. What would I do with all these pieces? I no longer wanted to be a victim of my pain and circumstances. No, I would use my pain to help others.

As I grieved, I did almost everything incorrectly. I imprisoned myself in an isolation cell, refusing phone calls and invitations. I didn't eat properly and lost too much weight. My energy level dropped to the point that I could only go to work and then straight home to bed.

When I finally realized that I couldn't continue like this and needed help, I became occupied with understanding the process and journey of grief. I needed a clear picture of what was happening to me.

I read about the stages of grief. I couldn't understand my grief in terms of stages. For instance, I never denied that Bill was dead. I wasn't in denial—I was numb. I blamed myself. I felt responsible.

I saw a counselor. She suggested I take a long bubble bath, light a candle, go for a walk, and enjoy a sunset. I could barely remember to shower but I tried the bubble bath and never felt more alone. I forgot to blow out the candle and almost burned the condo down. I didn't need a walk—I get enough outdoor exercise every day training my clients. I needed more than bubbles and sunsets.

I wondered why I was so ill-prepared to deal with grief. I wondered why people who knew me for years no longer knew how to act around me. Why are we all so awkward when it comes to grief especially when we know it's inevitable? Sometimes it's predictable yet we are conditioned not to think or talk about it. Why do we have to wait until we are at our most vulnerable to find the tools to help us deal with this life-altering crisis?

I was devastated I couldn't save Bill, but I was not going to let his suicide take me down with it. People still loved me and stood by me at my worst. It broke their hearts to witness my pain. I didn't have the tools to deal with my grief. I was determined to find those tools, and I did.

I don't want anyone else to go through the same painful experience unnecessarily when I could hand them the tools I'd been searching for.

This book is for you. You've been through a loss, but you haven't lost everything.

I sincerely wish that the tools in this book help you stay strong, heal with grace, and arrive on the other side of your turmoil with a new appreciation for life that makes the suffering a stepping stone to a more fulfilling existence—instead of a life sentence.

As you may know all too well, even something as basic as grocery shopping can feel like a Herculean task when you're grief-stricken. All I wanted was for someone to hand me a list of what to do and step-by-step instructions for how to do it. When your life suddenly goes sideways and everything feels as if it's up for grabs, you don't have the physical or psychic energy and space to make decisions about the small stuff. And you don't have to. I've made the lists and given you the steps, exercises, reminders, tips, meal plans, thought anchors, and instructions to help get you through this.

You owe it to yourself to focus on self-care and to make it your top priority. As they say before the plane takes off: *Put on your own oxygen mask before you try to help anyone else put on theirs!* You may not care about or value your well-being and health right now, but I know you will again.

And you'll be so glad you did!

PART TWO

YOUR PLAN FOR MOVING THROUGH GRIEF

Chapter Nine

Sleep

"Sleep is the best meditation."
—Dalai Lama

Sleep comes first in my guide because it's crucial for healing emotionally and physically. In fact, your healing *begins* with sleep. Be cognizant of the importance of a good night's sleep so that you will see it as a necessary tool in your grief journey. Grief and sleep can coexist, and adequate sleep for the griever is essential.

One of the most common physical responses to grief is low energy and trouble sleeping. Disruptions in your sleep patterns are very common in the first days, weeks, and months following a loss. However, grievers may find it difficult to stay awake. Typically, this results from added stress and depression.

There are lots of possible causes for sleep loss while you are grieving. Many of them are *secondary losses*. Secondary losses refer to losses other than the actual death or loss itself. They may include worrying about finances, sleeping and parenting solo, and taking on all kinds of responsibilities that your loved one always handled.

Everyone needs to get his or her sleep every night to function effectively every day. Sleep replenishes and repairs our bodies, our brains, and our immune systems. It keeps us going through difficult times when we are being challenged by stressful situations. At the same time, stress is often the main thing that keeps us awake at night. It robs us of those precious hours of sleep that will help us cope. The average adult requires seven to nine hours of sleep a night to function effectively. Too little sleep often results in illness, mood swings, fatigue, and an increase in accidents, memory loss, and depression.

Sleep deficiency also has been linked to depression, suicide, and risk-taking behavior. Ongoing sleep deficiency is linked to an increased risk of heart disease, kidney disease, high blood pressure, diabetes, and stroke. It can result in higher than normal blood sugar levels, which may increase your risk for diabetes. When you don't get enough sleep the hormones that make you feel hungry go up and the ones that make you feel full go down. This often leads to weight gain.

Lack of sleep can also lead to *microsleep*. Microsleep is brief moments of sleep that occur when you're normally awake. Examples are walking into the kitchen and not remembering why you're there, and driving somewhere and not remembering part of the trip.

Sleep helps your brain work properly. While you're sleeping your brain is forming new pathways to help you learn and remember information. Sleep deficiency alters activity in some parts of the brain so if you're sleep deficient you'll have trouble making decisions, solving problems, controlling your emotions, and coping with change.

Learning to get to sleep and staying asleep are important skills to learn while going through difficult times. Make it a priority to focus on getting your sleep rather than just lying awake, hoping that it will pass. It's crucial for physical renewal, hormonal regulation, and growth. When your brain is starved of sleep, concentrating on a single activity is challenging and multitasking is almost impossible. Sleep deprivation also takes a toll on decision-making ability.

Sleep is not a luxury—it's a *necessity.*

HOW TO SLEEP

The Bedroom

- Make sure your room is cool and dark.
- Install blackout curtains if your window treatments let too much light in.
- Purchase a sleep mask and even earplugs if you are sensitive to noise.
- Consider getting a new bed if yours is not comfortable. You spend a good portion of the day there, so don't feel the need to justify such a purchase.
- Purchase new sheets and maybe even a new comforter or duvet. Your bed is your sanctuary, and how it looks and feels to you makes a difference.

The Physical

- See your doctor and ask for a complete blood panel. A simple blood test could show a vitamin or mineral deficiency that could cause sleep problems.

- Remember that many prescription sleep aids can become habit forming and have many other side effects. Try not to use them if at all possible.
- Stick to a regular routine. Go to bed and get up at the same time each day, even on the weekends.
- Exercise during the day. Aerobic exercise such as a walk exposing you to natural light helps to contribute to a healthy sleep cycle, but don't engage in vigorous exercise after five p.m. Exercising earlier in the day helps wear you out. People who exercise regularly find it easier to fall and stay asleep.
- Receive therapeutic bodywork. Reiki, massage, or acupuncture will help you relax and bring your entire system back into balance, which in turn will help you sleep better.
- Watch what you eat in the evening. Do not eat anything within three hours of going to bed. If your body is busy digesting, it is hard for it to relax. Don't eat food high in sugar in the evening.
    - Avoid alcohol in the evenings. It may make you sleepy and you will fall asleep quickly after a couple glasses of wine, but you will wake up in the early morning hours while your liver is busy processing the alcohol and it will be hard to fall back to sleep.
    - Avoid caffeine after three in the afternoon.
    - Drink plenty of water during the day but not an hour before bed.
- Make a buffer time between electronic interfaces and bedtime. Cut off computer, phone, and television time and leave enough time for your bedtime rituals to wind down.
- Create nighttime rituals such as taking a soothing bath, reading a relaxing novel, or drinking warm milk—anything to signify to your brain that it's time to start unwinding.

- Surround yourself with soothing odors. Lavender is especially relaxing for most people. If you use it on your sheets, eventually you will associate it with relaxation and sleep.

THE MENTAL

- Practice relaxation exercises before going to bed. Yoga, deep breathing, or meditation can calm you down and transition your mind from your daily tasks to preparing to drift off.
- Discard your thoughts. Write down any nagging ideas or feelings you may have so you can deal with them tomorrow. Once you have captured them on paper, let them go.
- Practice relaxation techniques thirty minutes before bedtime. Use guided imagery or listen to natural sounds like ocean waves. Read, take a warm bath with Epsom salt, and drink decaffeinated hot herbal tea—all rituals that invite restful sleep.
- Perform a deep breathing relaxation routine in bed.
- Limit daytime naps to no longer than twenty minutes.
- If your spouse has died, sleep on their side of the bed. It will be easier for you if your own side is empty.
- During your grief journey you need to relax and rest more than usual. You may also find that you get tired easily, and that's okay. Be gentle with yourself, slow down, and do what is necessary to care for your body. Sleep is vital and should be tended to mindfully.
- You can always try counting sheep, but what works even better is getting into the habit of repeating *thought anchors*. (See below.)

THOUGHT ANCHORS

Thought anchors are affirmations, which help rewire your brain to reduce anxiety and cultivate deep relaxation. I like calling them "anchors" because they truly help moor you to a state of mind. You can say them or think them as long as you do so repeatedly. You do not need to have a calm mind to benefit from this practice.

Enjoy the way you feel in your bed. Imagine that all of the following thought anchors are true for you—right now in this moment—and enjoy the self-esteem relaxation you experience. Repeat each thought anchor in your mind or out loud with conviction.

Use the following thought anchors to help you relax and focus on building positive self-esteem:

- I am at peace with myself.
- I appreciate who I am.
- I value myself as a person.
- I deserve to be happy.
- When my mood is low, I accept my emotions and recognize that the low mood will pass, and I will be happy again.
- I look forward to the good times.
- My future is bright and positive.
- I look fondly upon many memories from my past.
- I am a good person, and I release the feelings of regret because I have learned and moved on.
- I have suffered enough, and now it is time to be free.
- I can move on and do good things.
- I feel good about who I am today.
- I eagerly develop new strengths.
- I enjoy being who I am, and love myself as I am.
- I handle difficulties with grace.
- I deserve time for myself, and I feel good about taking this time regularly.
- I allow myself to experience and express emotions, both negative and positive.

- I accept I can't change my past. I have grown from my experiences and look forward to a happy future.

HOW I SLEEP

The first few months after Bill's death, I couldn't get a decent night's sleep. As a result, I walked around in a fog unable to make even the smallest of decisions.

After months of sleepless nights, I figured out which methods helped me get back on track and feel refreshed after an uninterrupted night of sleep. The first thing I did was stop stressing about sleep. Lying in bed worrying about how awful the next day without Bill was exhausting and created more anxiety. Instead, I focused on changing my perspective on sleep. Changing all the negative thoughts about my inability to sleep helped to reduce some of the stress, which was causing my insomnia. I realized that I was exaggerating the problem, and if I was extremely tired the next day, I simply carved out a time to relax during the day. It wasn't that big of a deal.

Now if I can't fall asleep after twenty minutes at bedtime, I get out of bed and read, meditate or speak thought anchors out loud, or write. I never allow myself to turn on my computer, phone, or TV.

I learned to leave my day behind me. I typically write down thoughts that are causing me stress before bed, and then allow myself to forget about them. My journal is always there the next morning to help me pick up where I left off. This nighttime ritual has helped me break the cycle of linking my bed to negative thoughts.

I only go to bed when I'm truly exhausted. This eliminates the time spent tossing and turning when you're only faintly tired.

I cut back on my caffeine consumption in the morning. My anxiety level and blood pressure were extremely high, and the caffeine only made that situation worse.

I use guided imagery to help me get to sleep. The Body Scan Meditation (see Chapter Thirteen) helps me to quiet my mind and body. I use this to unwind, and repeat in the morning to create a sense of calmness to start my day.

I limit my afternoon nap to twenty minutes to ensure I could sleep at night. I would wake up energized. The short power nap helped keep my performance going strong the rest of the day. I find it more effective, and certainly healthier, than a cup of coffee! In the past, I used sleep as an escape. After lying down in the afternoon and napping for one hour or more, I'd wake up and feel worse.

I had my doctor do a complete blood panel and discovered I was deficient in magnesium and vitamin D. I thought my blood panel would show I was in perfect health because I'm a fitness professional who has always followed a very strict, healthy diet . . . but this was not the case. I now take magnesium supplements because magnesium is essential for sleep problems. It is vital for the function of GABA receptors, which exist across all areas of the brain and nervous system. GABA is a combining neurotransmitter that the brain needs to switch off and rest. Without it, I was tense, and my thoughts would race as I would lie in bed staring at the ceiling. I take 500 mg of magnesium before I go to sleep. This has made a remarkable difference in my ability to get a good night's rest.

I also take 600 IUs of vitamin D per day and have noticed an increase in energy and my overall sense of well-being. At bedtime, I take 20 mg of melatonin, a hormone made by the pineal gland in the brain that helps control sleeping and waking cycles. My body clock controls how much melatonin my body makes. Light affects how much melatonin our bodies produce. My natural melatonin level has slowly dropped with age.

I don't suggest you start taking any of these supplements simply because I take them, but you should be aware of what is available and do your research. Discuss them with someone who can interpret your blood work and see what supplements may help you sleep. Try consulting a naturopathic doctor whose practice includes holistic methods.

Chapter Ten

Eat

"Let food be thy medicine and medicine be thy food."
—Hippocrates

After the death of a loved one—particularly after a sudden or unexpected death—it is not unusual to suffer from what is known as *decision fatigue*. This is when the quality of your decisions deteriorates because you've had to make many decisions in a short period.

Decision fatigue enables poor and irrational choices: Your willpower is tapped. You don't have enough energy to resist impulses for quick-fix satisfaction solutions that often make you feel worse.

Making lists may help mitigate decision fatigue, particularly when it comes to mundane tasks such as grocery shopping. The more you can limit the small decisions you need to make, the more energy and focus you'll have to make larger, more important decisions as you move forward in your journey.

Copy the next few pages or rip them out and tuck them into your wallet. Simply cross off items from each category below, and you'll always have something nutritious in your fridge and pantry to eat—even and perhaps most especially when you don't feel like eating.

It's helpful to break your list into categories so you cover all the necessary nutrition you need without having to think about it. Quantity will depend on how many people there are in your household.

During this difficult time, stress is probably a part of your life, but it doesn't have to lead to weight gain. When you are stressed, your body releases heavy amounts of *cortisol*, a hormone that contributes to weight gain especially around the midsection. If you find yourself reaching for high-fat, sugary snacks when you feel stressed, you are not alone. But you can break the cycle, and you don't have to give in to those urges. Focus on making better food choices.

You must never allow yourself to become too hungry. When go too long without eating, your blood sugar drops. It is hard to think rationally with low blood sugar, and soon you'll eat anything you can get your hands on. Don't skip meals, even if you don't feel hungry. Eat healthy snacks to avoid becoming too hungry between meals. Choose snacks high in protein because it takes longer for the body to digest them, which makes you feel full longer. Avoid snacks high in fat and sugar. Keep healthy food in the house or at work so you don't need to rely on fast food or the vending machine.

Plan ahead what you will order if you are going to eat out at a restaurant. You can look at menus online for most restaurants so you can plan ahead and stick to your plan.

Keep portion size in mind. When you are under stress it is easy to eat without thinking, which leads to overeating. Smaller portions will help keep calorie intake under control. Stay hydrated by drinking water.

Gaining weight is not unusual for people in stressful situations, but if left unchecked, soon the weight gain itself will become a source of additional stress. Not being able to fit into your clothes or looking in the mirror and seeing yourself gaining weight is no fun. Your weight can shoot up quickly. Stay in control and make a plan to eat healthy.

If you do gain weight, be sure to lose it safely through a healthy diet and exercise. Even though losing a few pounds because of stress may seem like a bonus in the short term, it's not. Losing weight quickly during times of heightened anxiety and stress can also mean you're not getting the vital nutrients your body needs to fuel your brain, nervous system, muscles, and everything else that keeps you healthy. Eventually this leads to poor health and illness.

This is not what you need during a difficult time. You need good nutrition to help you think clearly, stay strong, and feel healthy during your most challenging times, even if making smart choices about what you consume is difficult.

HOW TO EAT

- Prepare some emergency frozen meals in advance. Cook as much food as you can that you can freeze, portion it out in Ziploc bags, or store it in Tupperware. When you have low energy, you can just pull it out of the freezer and stick it in the microwave.
- When you are low in energy, doing dishes at the end of a meal seems overwhelming. Learn to make meals in one pot and use paper plates, bowls, and plastic utensils.
- Ask for help if you need it.

- Ask a family member or friend to go grocery shopping with you and help you with some basic meal prep.
- Make cooking a self-care event.
- Cooking can be very creative and relaxing and can help take your mind off your anxiety and depression. Put on some soothing background music and do your best to make it engaging.
- Get your groceries delivered from your local store or through an online service.
- Invite someone over to eat with you. A guest whose company you enjoy and whom you trust to be present with you will certainly make you feel more motivated to prepare a healthy meal.
- Having simple, healthy readily available recipes makes it so you don't have to think too hard about it. When you're feeling a bit more energetic, searching for and reading new recipes can inspire you. (I've included a five-day meal plan in this chapter to help you get started.)
- Forgive yourself for the bad days. Don't punish yourself for making unhealthy food choices. Eating healthy is a marathon—not a race!—so one day of bad choices is nothing to feel ashamed about. Food is there to make you feel strong and healthy.
- Healthy food creates a healthy mood so you are much less tempted to reach for sugary foods or alcohol when you feel stressed.
- Eat real food, not processed food. Choose fresh or frozen vegetables and steam them or toss them in a salad. Cook a lean cut of meat, fish, or chicken. Have fresh fruit for dessert. Choose nuts, fruit, or seeds as a snack.
- Stay away from foods that come in boxes and cans, even if they seem easier to prepare. They are more expensive and less healthy.

- Cut back on caffeine. Switch to herbal tea. Save the sugary desserts, sodas, alcohol, and white breads and cereals for another time and another place. You don't need them in your life right now.
- Tear out the lists on the next few pages or take photos of them using your phone so that you always have them with you when you are at the grocery store. These lists will help you from having to think about what to buy or cook. You can make quick smoothies, protein-filled snacks, and healthy meals by keeping the items listed below in stock—no matter the season.

GROCERY LIST

Vegetables

- Lettuce, one head or one bag
- Broccoli, two frozen bags
- Zucchini, two
- Asparagus, one bundle
- Onions, three yellow, one red
- Bell peppers, four
- Spinach, two frozen bags
- Tomatoes, four
- Beans, two cans
- Potatoes, three sweet, three white

Fruits

- Apples, four
- Berries, two frozen bags
- Oranges, four
- Grapefruit, four

Protein

- Skinless chicken breasts, four half breasts
- Eggs, one dozen
- Pork tenderloin, 6 ounces
- Lean ground turkey, 2.5 pounds
- Sliced turkey, half a pound
- Fresh salmon, one filet
- Tuna, two cans packed in water
- Shrimp, 16-ounce frozen bag
- Almond and peanut butter, one jar
- Nuts, two bags, almonds, Brazil nuts, walnuts, or pistachios
- Lentils, one bag

Dairy

- Reduced fat mozzarella and feta cheese, one package
- Milk, one carton unsweetened almond
- Low-fat Greek yogurt, five single containers
- Cottage cheese, 16 ounces

Whole Grains

- Whole-grain bread, one loaf
- Whole-grain cereal, one box
- Whole-grain waffles, one box
- Quinoa shell pasta
- Oatmeal, one container long cooking

Condiments

- Garlic
- Lemon
- Dijon mustard
- Salsa

- Low-calorie salad dressing
- Marinara sauce
- Vinegar
- Olive oil

Supplies

- BPA-free food storage containers
- Disposable foil pans
- Sandwich bags
- Airtight containers
- Paper plates
- Plastic forks and spoons

FIVE-DAY MEAL PLAN

MONDAY

- Breakfast: Egg, spinach, and feta cheese scramble
- Lunch: Large salad with turkey
- Snack: Apple with almond butter
- Dinner: Turkey spinach burger with or without the bun. Sweet potato and mixed green salad with dressing

Tuesday

- Breakfast: Berry protein smoothie, blend berries, banana, almond milk, and peanut butter
- Lunch: Turkey sandwich with mustard, tomatoes, and lettuce. Grapefruit slices
- Snack: Orange and 12 nuts
- Dinner: Lemon garlic shrimp with sautéed spinach and baked sweet potato

Wednesday

- Breakfast: Whole-grain cereal or oatmeal with almond milk and fruit
- Lunch: Open-faced tuna melt with mozzarella
- Snack: Apple and 12 nuts
- Dinner: Chicken quinoa pasta with marinara sauce

Thursday

- Breakfast: Salsa scramble sandwich
- Lunch: Open-faced peanut butter banana sandwich with carrots and bell pepper sticks
- Snack: Lettuce pepper turkey roll-ups, sliced turkey wrapped around asparagus and bell pepper sticks
- Dinner: Baked fish with steamed broccoli and baked potato with salsa or Greek yogurt topping

Friday

- Breakfast: Waffles with almond butter and sliced banana
- Lunch: Lentil bean salad
- Snack: Greek yogurt and 12 nuts
- Dinner: Pork tenderloin, baked potato topped with Greek yogurt and carrots

WHAT I EAT

After Bill's suicide, my body and mind were shaken to the core. My normal healthy eating habits and gym routine went out the window. I spent hours lying in bed with a quiet sadness that left me feeling numb. All of this was a reflection of what was happening to me inwardly and outwardly.

It wasn't so much that I didn't want to eat—it just never entered my mind. It wasn't important anymore. I was too busy mourning the loss of my husband and thinking about him.

My weight loss began a few months before Bill's death because I was in survival mode trying to help him. The only time I would remember to eat was when my blood sugar would get so low that I began to feel lightheaded.

I received many compliments at Bill's memorial service—people told me how great I looked. But I did not look healthy because I wasn't! I had lost about fifteen pounds, most of it muscle. My face looked drawn and a decade older than I actually was. I felt extremely weak. I just wanted to crawl into bed and pull the covers over my head.

It took me well over six months to resume my regular exercise routine and get on a healthy eating plan. Although I no longer make the elaborate healthy meals I did for Bill and myself in the past, each Sunday I sit down and plan what I will eat for the week and make sure I have healthy snacks available all day, every day.

Typically, I cook salmon, chicken, or ground turkey marinara sauce with a whole grain or quinoa penne pasta. I use the pasta sparingly, heavier on the sauce. I freeze the leftovers and repeat the meal throughout the week. I add spinach, broccoli, bell peppers, and other frozen veggies to revive it as needed. Turkey chili is another favorite I often fix when the weather cools off. Both of these satisfying dinners can be frozen and microwaved in minutes.

Just as I schedule my hourly clients on a daily basis, I schedule my caloric intake and what I will eat and when I will eat it. The key to maintaining a healthy body is structure and planning. I don't buy foods high in sugar or that have no nutritional value. This eliminates the temptation to overeat or binge. If you can't see it, you can't eat it!

Some of my favorite go-to high-protein snacks include hard-boiled eggs, single-serving cottage cheese, peanut butter packs, sliced cheese or string cheese, roasted chickpeas, Greek yogurt, turkey roll-ups, almonds, tuna pouches, kefir, and edamame.

I know what healthy snacks work for me and keep them handy in my purse, workout bag, on the kitchen counter, in my desk, and in the glove compartment of my car.

Even when I don't feel like it, I make meal planning a part of my life with the intention of improving my overall physical and mental health. I feel better, look better, and am stronger—and ready to face whatever life throws at me.

Chapter Eleven

Move

"Change happens through movement and movement heals."
—Joseph Pilates

When you are in the midst of your grief, exercising is probably the last thing you want to do. But exercise will make a big difference in how you feel. It is a powerful depression fighter as it promotes all kinds of changes in your brain—including neural growth, reduced inflammation, and new activity patterns that promote feelings of calm and well-being.

Exercise releases endorphins, which are powerful chemicals in your brain that energize your mood. It also helps to relax your muscles and relieve tension. When your body feels better, so does your mind.

Working out will definitely help ease symptoms of anxiety or depression, lower your blood pressure, and help prevent a wide range of diseases. The psychological and emotional benefits are extremely important as you need to get away from the cycle of negative thoughts you may be experiencing as a result of your loss.

Some common barriers you may be experiencing right now such as exhaustion or extreme stress are to be expected. Regular exercise is one of the most effective ways to improve your mental health. It helps you relieve stress, improve your memory, and help you sleep as well as boost your overall mood. This is exactly what you need right now!

HOW TO MOVE

- Any activity that gets you moving is good. Cycling, walking, dancing, whatever—just make sure it's something you enjoy so that you'll stick with it. If you find an activity a chore, you'll find every excuse in the book to skip it.
- You can reap all the physical and mental health benefits of exercise with thirty minutes of moderate exercise five times a week. Two fifteen-minute or even three ten-minute exercise sessions are also an option. If that seems like too much, even just a few minutes of physical activity are better than none at all. Start with five- or ten-minute sessions and slowly increase your time. Chances are that once you get started, you'll be able to go longer than you think.
- Don't be a slave to your scale! You're in survival mode right now so do what you can to raise your endorphins.
- Try to do some resistance exercises with weights or even your body weight. Lunges, squats, push-ups, and dips are some examples. Having more muscle increases your metabolic rate twenty-four hours a day, whether you are exercising or not.

- Anyone can starve and dehydrate themselves for a few weeks and see big changes on the scale, but such changes are temporary and unhealthy. The more muscle you have, the more energy you will use, even at rest. Remember also that muscle weighs more than fat, so an increase in weight could be an increase in your muscle mass.
- Think of exercise as a lifestyle rather than just a task to cross off on your daily checklist. It may be a good idea to exercise with a friend or family member rather than working out alone. Right now, the companionship may be just as important as the exercise. Call a friend and ask them to join you for a walk or attend an exercise class you both might enjoy.
- Try to exercise at the time of day when your energy is at its highest. That might be first thing in the morning, at a lunch break, or after work. As you begin to make moving a part of your daily routine and start to feel better, you will experience a greater sense of control over your entire well-being.

Physical activity is a powerful energizer. If you're feeling overwhelmed, hopeless, or experiencing low self-esteem, remember that any form of physical activity helps you do everything else better. Train yourself to think of physical activity as your priority, and you'll be amazed how you find time to fit it into your busy schedule.

HOW I MOVE

I have been in the fitness industry for more than thirty years. I have taught every trend from high- and low-impact aerobics, step aerobics, spinning, Pilates, and everything in between.

What works for me now is moderation. I do a balance of strength-training exercises through my Pilates workouts, yoga, and cardio training. I run four miles four times a week for my fat burning program. I'm not a big fan of large gyms and weight training.

I don't have the same energy level as I had in the past. This could be a result of just getting older, but I think being under incredible stress played a part in it. I'm consistent about my workouts but if some days I just can't muster up the energy, that's okay too. Occasionally I cut myself some slack and just allow extra time for sleeping, reading, or meditating.

Exercise helps me combat stress. Not only does it increase my endorphins, but it also gets me into the groove of keeping my mind off things causing me stress. Because the increase in endorphins improves my mood, I'm better equipped to handle potentially stressful situations and start my day with a positive attitude.

I work out in the morning or early afternoon. These workouts leave me feeling more energetic and productive for the rest of the day. If it's not possible to exercise early, a midday workout is an effective pick-me-up too. If I exercise too close to bedtime, it has the opposite effect and I have trouble falling asleep.

I spend about fifteen minutes every morning practicing six to ten yoga poses (also called *asanas*). Many of the asanas at the end of this chapter are particularly helpful for grief. Specifically, they are *heart-openers*, which are believed to have emotional, psychological, spiritual, and physical benefits. You don't need prior yoga experience to try these! They will help you relax and gently stretch your muscles.

Through the combination of cardio workouts, strength training using a Pilates reformer, and yoga, I've found a combination of activities that I enjoy; this is the key to my overall health and fitness.

Exercise improves life expectancy as much as quitting smoking does. It has improved my life in so many ways, which convinces me to keep it a priority. In fact, I can't remember the last time I had a cold! My mood is significantly improved on the days I exercise. After I work out, I'm so much more content and grateful for my health and body.

YOGA POSES FOR GRIEF

Child's Pose

Kneel on the floor. Touch your big toes together. Sit on your heels. Separate your knees about as wide as your hips. Put your palms on the floor and stretch out your arms. You may also rest your forehead on the floor if that feels good to you.

Cat Cow

Cat Cow is really two warm-up poses to help you stretch and prepare for the other poses. Create a "flow" by going back and forth between the two poses—always inhaling for cow and exhaling for cat.

For cow pose, inhale as you drop your belly toward the mat. Lift your chin and chest, and gently gaze up at the ceiling.

For cat pose, exhale as you draw your belly to your spine and around your back toward the ceiling. The pose is reminiscent of a cat stretching its back.

Warrior 2

Warrior 2 enhances strength, stability, and concentration. It will help you stretch your legs, groin, and chest. It can even relieve backaches, stimulate healthy digestion, improve breathing capacity, and increase circulation. Simply exhale as you step your feet apart, and look down to make sure your heels are aligned with one another. Your front foot should be pointing directly forward, and your back foot should be at a forty-five-degree angle. If possible, the knee of your front foot should be directly lined up with the ankle below it. Try to stay directly above your hips—don't lean too forward or backward. Stay in this pose for a minute, breathing slowly in and out. Make sure to do Warrior 2 on your opposite side.

Humble Warrior

Coming from Warrior 2, shorten your stance one to two feet and clasp your hands together. Slowly lower your chest forward as far as you can—don't overextend yourself. Release your head and neck, and allow your hands to gently drift up. Feel the stretch in your shoulders, neck, and chest. Carefully rise out of this pose, switch feet, and do the same on the other side. Be careful practicing this pose if you have neck or shoulder problems.

Camel

Camel is a back-bending pose that stretches the entire front of the body and helps improve spinal flexibility while strengthening the back muscles and improving posture. Begin on your knees with your knees no farther apart than your hips. Support your lower back by resting your hands on it with your fingertips pointing toward the floor. Lean back slowly and stop when you feel a gentle tug in your chest.

If you feel comfortable and want to go deeper, reach for your heels with your hands. Whether you follow the first or second modification, inhale and exhale very slowly for thirty to sixty seconds. Be careful coming out of the pose. Lift your torso by pushing your hips toward the floor, and let your head come up last. Sit back on your heels and close your eyes as you allow the blood flow to come back down. Go back into child's pose and rest. Do not try camel pose if you have any back issues.

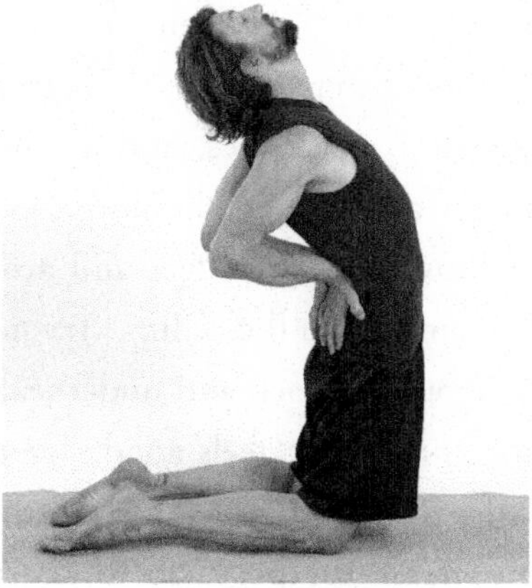

Sphinx

If camel pose is too hard on your back, try *sphinx*, which is a beginning backbend that helps to open the chest, lungs, and lower back. It also strengthens the spine and soothes the nervous system. Begin by lying face down on the floor with your legs extended behind you. Keep your legs hips-width apart and the tops of your feet flat on the mat. With your forearms on the floor, bring your arms up and rest your elbows directly under your shoulders. Keep your forearms parallel to one another and your fingertips pointing forward. Drop your shoulder blades down your back and gently draw your chest forward. Slightly draw your chin up and let your face and eyes soften. Inhale and exhale at least ten times each.

Bridge

Bridge pose is considered a mild *inversion*, which is when your heart is higher than your head. Benefits of inversions include relief from stress, insomnia, fatigue, mild depression, headaches, and anxiety. Lie on your back with your knees bent and feet on the floor. Your legs should be no wider than your hips. Press your feet and arms into the floor, and exhale as you lift your hips to the ceiling. Try not to squeeze your buttocks. Roll your shoulders back and underneath your body, and clasp your hands together if that feels good. Try to keep your weight evenly distributed between your feet. Hold this pose up to one minute. When you release the pose, do so slowly by rolling your vertebrae one by one to the floor, and exhale as you unravel. Do not perform this pose if you have any issues with your neck or shoulders.

Legs up the Wall

Legs up the Wall helps you ease into a state of relaxation and renewal. It's a very useful pose if you have mild backache. Start by lying on your back. You can literally put your legs up a wall by scooting your buttocks up to the wall and raising your feet—thus allowing the wall to support your legs—or simply raise your legs until they are directly above your hips. Do whatever is most comfortable for you.

Supine Twist

Supine Twist stimulates and detoxifies your organs and decompresses and wrings out your anxiety. It restores balance, stretches your back muscles and glutes, and massages your back and hips. Begin by lying on the floor, inhaling, extending your left leg, and keeping the right leg drawn tightly to your chest. Extend your right arm, and as you exhale, use your left hand to draw your right knee over your body. The goal is not to touch your knee to the floor, so don't force your knee too far. Let the weight of your knee fall so that your back gently twists. Be sure to do the same on the other side.

Savasana

Every yoga sequence or flow should end with *savasana.* No matter how many poses you choose to do, be sure to give yourself at least two to five minutes at the end of savasana. Many yoga teachers believe that this is the most important pose of your practice because it renews the body, spirit, and mind. Begin by lying on your back with your legs straight, your arms at your sides, and your palms facing up. Let your breath occur naturally. If you feel like spreading your arms and legs out, do it. Relax your face and body, release your tongue from the roof of your mouth, and let your body melt into the ground. When you exit the pose, bring gentle movement and awareness back into your hands and feet, then roll to one side and rest for a moment before inhaling and pressing yourself up to a seat.

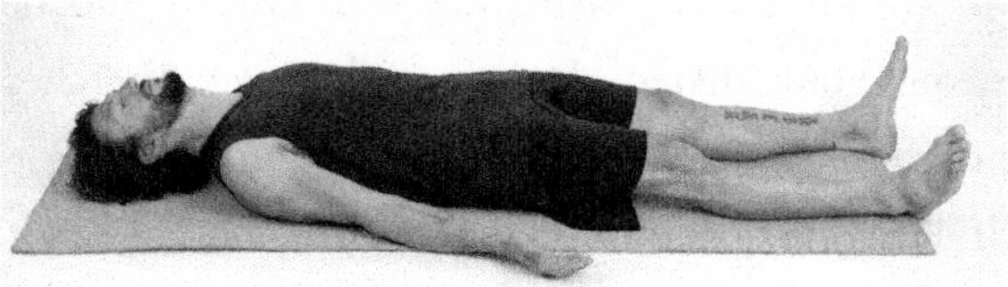

Chapter Twelve

Do

"Start by doing what's necessary; then do what's possible; and suddenly you are doing the impossible."

—Francis of Assisi

We all have daily routines that bring structure to our days and give us a sense of stability and security. If you are suffering any type of loss, your daily routine suddenly ceases to exist. The stability and security you once relied on has vanished and been replaced with chaos and fear.

Establish a new routine and create structures you can rely on as quickly as possible. This will give you time to focus on other issues that are essential to your recovery.

Start by making *lists* of things that need to be done every day. You may now have to handle the finances, taxes, laundry, cooking, and other responsibilities that require learning new skills. Not only did you lose your loved one, but you are now responsible for all of the things that he or she used to handle. It may take months until your new routine feels normal. That's okay.

Create the structure and stick to it. Write down even the smallest tasks while you're learning to cope with your new life. Cross them off when you accomplish them.

On the following pages are blank lists for each day of the week. Use these as a guide for setting up your routine. Write in the pages of this book. Make copies of the pages and tape them to the door of your bedroom closet, or stick them to the fridge with a magnet. Tear them out. Do whatever works for you to establish a routine and order that will make moving through grief easier and doable.

MONDAY

Date: ____________

Daily Tasks:

☐
☐
☐
☐
☐
☐
☐
☐
☐
☐
☐

Appointments/Errands:

☐
☐
☐
☐
☐
☐

Healthy Habits:

Water Intake (circle each 8 oz. serving)

1 2 3 4 5 6 7 8 9 10 11 12 13 14 15

Exercise (what and duration):

Weekly Chores:

☐
☐
☐
☐
☐
☐
☐
☐

To-Do List:

☐
☐
☐
☐
☐
☐
☐
☐
☐

Meal Menu:

☐
☐
☐
☐
☐
☐

TUESDAY

Date: ____________

Daily Tasks:

☐
☐
☐
☐
☐
☐
☐
☐
☐
☐
☐

Appointments/Errands:

☐
☐
☐
☐
☐
☐

Healthy Habits:

Water Intake (circle each 8 oz. serving)

1 2 3 4 5 6 7 8 9 10 11 12 13 14 15

Exercise (what and duration):

Weekly Chores:

☐
☐
☐
☐
☐
☐
☐
☐

To-Do List:

☐
☐
☐
☐
☐
☐
☐
☐
☐

Meal Menu:

☐
☐
☐
☐
☐
☐

WEDNESDAY

Date: ____________

Daily Tasks:

- ☐
- ☐
- ☐
- ☐
- ☐
- ☐
- ☐
- ☐
- ☐
- ☐
- ☐

Appointments/Errands:

- ☐
- ☐
- ☐
- ☐
- ☐
- ☐

Healthy Habits:

Water Intake (circle each 8 oz. serving)

1 2 3 4 5 6 7 8 9 10 11 12 13 14 15

Exercise (what and duration):

Weekly Chores:

- ☐
- ☐
- ☐
- ☐
- ☐
- ☐
- ☐
- ☐

To-Do List:

- ☐
- ☐
- ☐
- ☐
- ☐
- ☐
- ☐
- ☐
- ☐

Meal Menu:

- ☐
- ☐
- ☐
- ☐
- ☐
- ☐

THURSDAY

Date: ____________

Daily Tasks:

☐
☐
☐
☐
☐
☐
☐
☐
☐
☐
☐

Appointments/Errands:

☐
☐
☐
☐
☐
☐

Healthy Habits:

Water Intake (circle each 8 oz. serving)

1 2 3 4 5 6 7 8 9 10 11 12 13 14 15

Exercise (what and duration):

Weekly Chores:

☐
☐
☐
☐
☐
☐
☐
☐

To-Do List:

☐
☐
☐
☐
☐
☐
☐
☐
☐

Meal Menu:

☐
☐
☐
☐
☐
☐

FRIDAY

Date: ___________

Daily Tasks:

☐
☐
☐
☐
☐
☐
☐
☐
☐
☐
☐

Weekly Chores:

☐
☐
☐
☐
☐
☐
☐
☐

To-Do List:

☐
☐
☐
☐
☐
☐
☐
☐
☐

Appointments/Errands:

☐
☐
☐
☐
☐
☐

Healthy Habits:

Water Intake (circle each 8 oz. serving)

1 2 3 4 5 6 7 8 9 10 11 12 13 14 15

Exercise (what and duration):

Meal Menu:

☐
☐
☐
☐
☐
☐

SATURDAY

Date: ____________

Daily Tasks:

- ☐
- ☐
- ☐
- ☐
- ☐
- ☐
- ☐
- ☐
- ☐
- ☐
- ☐

Appointments/Errands:

- ☐
- ☐
- ☐
- ☐
- ☐
- ☐

Healthy Habits:

Water Intake (circle each 8 oz. serving)

1 2 3 4 5 6 7 8 9 10 11 12 13 14 15

Exercise (what and duration):

Weekly Chores:

- ☐
- ☐
- ☐
- ☐
- ☐
- ☐
- ☐
- ☐

To-Do List:

- ☐
- ☐
- ☐
- ☐
- ☐
- ☐
- ☐
- ☐
- ☐

Meal Menu:

- ☐
- ☐
- ☐
- ☐
- ☐
- ☐

SUNDAY

Date: ____________

Daily Tasks:

☐
☐
☐
☐
☐
☐
☐
☐
☐
☐
☐

Appointments/Errands:

☐
☐
☐
☐
☐
☐

Healthy Habits:

Water Intake (circle each 8 oz. serving)
1 2 3 4 5 6 7 8 9 10 11 12 13 14 15

Exercise (what and duration):

Weekly Chores:

☐
☐
☐
☐
☐
☐
☐
☐

To-Do List:

☐
☐
☐
☐
☐
☐
☐
☐
☐

Meal Menu:

☐
☐
☐
☐
☐
☐

WHAT TO DO

- **Prioritize your list.** Use A, B, and C and place them next to items on your list to prioritize tasks that must be done immediately (A), things that should be done soon (B), and things that need to be done eventually (C). This will help you plan your time when looking at a long to-do list.
- **Delegate as much as possible.** When friends and family ask how they can help you, take out your list and figure out what they would be able to do, at least in the short term. They really do want to help. Also, review the list for things you can pay someone else to do.
- **Resume activities that you enjoy.** You may not want to return to leisure-time activities yet, but you should get back to having some enjoyment as soon as possible. Look for new and different activities where you may meet new people. Stretch your imagination. You need a change of scenery, schedule it. Put it on your list.
- **Learn a new skill.** Learning something new will keep your mind busy and make you feel accomplished. Maybe there was something you always wanted to do that you never could find time for before. Make sure it requires daily practice and enjoy checking it off your list.

WHAT I DO

For years, my days had begun with Bill bringing me coffee in bed, turning on the television news, and giving me a kiss as he headed off to work.

After his death, I learned to set the timer on the coffeemaker. I stopped starting my day with the litany of doom and gloom that is listening to the news and now begin the day in silence. I do my daily chores, check my email, and schedule my early clients. I don't dwell on my old routine. I have a new life and with that, a new routine.

I stepped up my game as a small-business owner, found a new location for my Pilates studio, and did everything I could to promote it. I assumed all of Bill's household chores. When I do forget to do something here and there, I am not hard on myself. After all, I've been through a lot.

I've had to assume all the responsibilities that Bill had handled while he was alive, and although it took me awhile, I soon got up to speed.

Below are two examples of lists I made. I created the first one shortly after Bill died and wrote the second list one year later. You'll see that they're very different!

FRIDAY

Date: 10-12-12

Daily Tasks:

- A. call Fairhaven Memorial ☐
- A. Call venues: ☐
  - a. Chart House ☐
  - b. Cannon's ☐
  - c. Marine Inst. ☐
- ☐
- A. Call Saddleback ☐
- ☐
- A. Feed Smoke, litterbox ☐
- ☐
- ☐
- ☐

Weekly Chores:

- B. get groceries ☐
- ☐
- C. clean, vacuum ☐
- ☐
- B. take out garbage ☐
- ☐
- A. get gas ☐

To Do List:

- A. Deposit, venue ☐
- A. pastor for service ☐
- B. post memorial info ☐
- C. buy some clothes ☐
- C. call Susie – flowers ☐
- C. call Vince, Ken, Carlow – speakers ☐
- ☐
- ☐
- ☐
- ☐
- ☐

Appointments/Errands:

- A. Chart House – 1pm Mon.
- ☐
- A. Cannon's 3pm Mon. ☐
- ☐
- A. Saddleback 11am Wed. ☐
- ☐
- ☐

Healthy Habits:

Water Intake (circle each 8 oz serving)

1 2 3 (4) 5 6 7 8 9 10 11 12 13 14 15

Exercise (what and duration):

Meal Menu:

take out:

- A. Kaleyard ☐
- B. The Point ☐
- C. Pizza ☐
- ☐
- ☐

MONDAY

Date: 10-14-13

Daily Tasks:

A. Pilates Clients: ☐
8, 9, 10 3:30, 4:30 ☐
A. Grief Clients: ☐
11, 12 ☐
B. Trader Joes-groceries ☐
A. Garbage Day ☐
B. Confirm Tues. Clients ☐

Appointments/Errands:

B. Haircut - 2pm Fri. ☐
A. Smoke - Vet - 3pm Wed ☐
A. Dr. appt. 1:30 Thurs ☐

Healthy Habits:

Water Intake (circle each 8 oz. serving)

1 2 3 4 5 6 7 8 9 (10) 11 12 13 14 15

Exercise (what and duration):

A. pilates, 1hr. M, W, F, Sat.
A. run - Tues, Fri Sun. (4 miles.)

Weekly Chores:

C. vacuum, clean ☐
A. fill hummingbird feeder ☐
B. laundry, wash bedding ☐
B. water plants ☐
B. car wash, gas ☐

To Do List:

B. Ralphs, groceries ☐
B. answer emails ☐
A. bank deposit ☐
A. pay bills ☐
A. renew lease ☐
C. buy sheets ☐
A. computer service ☐
B. blog ☐
A. call client inquiries ☐

Meal Menu:

Breakfasts: - smoothie ☐
Lunch: - salads, chicken, tuna, egg ☐
Dinner: - salmon pasta ☐
Snacks: almonds, apples

Chapter Thirteen

Breathe

"Breathe. Let go. And remind yourself that this very moment is the only one you know you have for sure."
—Oprah

Breathing is vitally important, yet most of us never notice we're doing it. Observing each inhale and exhale as it occurs will help you anchor yourself to the present moment. This present moment is where you will find peace.

As you learn to breathe properly, you may notice a decrease in your blood pressure: Proper breathing reduces your stress level and calms you. When this happens, all those triggers that normally draw you deeper into grief will become less stressful. Learning to breathe and relax is one of the most important keys to growing calmer and more peaceful as you work your way through grief.

Our thoughts, senses, emotions, and physical body are interconnected. They rely on each other for feedback and signals, and they react accordingly. It has been proven scientifically that if you are watching a television program that makes you laugh, your levels of *cortisol* and *epinephrine*—the stress hormones—will decrease. The production of antibodies in your immune system will increase too.

The opposite is true when you're experiencing a stressful period that causes anxiety, unhappiness, or sadness: You become at risk for hormone imbalances that can jeopardize your health and long-term psychological well-being.

Proper breathing transforms energy from tension to relaxation by turning off our sympathetic nervous system, which produces stress hormones while turning on our parasympathetic nervous system. It lowers blood pressure, decreases heart rate, and creates a sense of calm. It can help alleviate depression by restoring balance to the biochemistry of the brain. The feel-good hormones *oxytocin* and *prolactin* increase as the level of the stress hormone *cortisol* decreases.

Of course, you can't sit in front of the TV all day to keep your mind off of your problems, but tools are available to help control your physical reaction to stressors during your day. Having those tools at your disposal will go a long way toward keeping you physically and mentally healthy.

Be kind to yourself as you learn how to practice proper breathing through meditation and other techniques suggested below. If at first the practice seems difficult, don't fret—stay with it.

For starters, you may want to sit quietly for a few minutes. Don't *do* anything. Just sit. Even a few minutes sitting will help calm your mind and body, which, over time, will help you embrace, examine, and release your grief. Eventually you will find that the pain subsides and you actually experience moments of happiness.

In your own time, grief will no longer control you. It will sit quietly in your mind next to moments of joy, which will allow you to honor the love you have for the person you are grieving.

Breathing will help you get to that place.

Find a practice that works for you.

HOW TO BREATHE

Deep Breathing

1. Find a quiet, comfortable place for a few minutes. Sit up straight with your hands by your sides or on top of your legs, palms up or down—whichever feels most natural and relaxed.
2. Close your eyes; breathe deeply through your nose so that your abdomen expands first, followed by your chest for a count of four.
3. Hold your breath for a count of eight.
4. Slowly exhale completely through your mouth, making a whooshing sound to the count of twelve.
5. Repeat four times.
6. Open your eyes. Breathe normally. Take a minute before standing to make sure you are not lightheaded.

Visualization

1. Find a place to sit comfortably with your eyes closed.
2. Think of a specific place you can visit in your mind—a spot you find peaceful and comforting. It can be inside or outside, real or imaginary. Whatever place works for you and evokes calm, peace, safety, and happiness—go there in your mind.
3. Now use your senses to describe silently to yourself what you are experiencing. What do you hear? What do you smell? What do you see? What do you taste? How does your skin feel?

4. Relax and enjoy this place in your imagination for as long as you like. When you are ready, slowly open your eyes and come back to the here and now.

Compassion Meditation:[1]

1. Begin by sitting quietly in a comfortable position. Keep your hands resting on your legs, knees, or by your sides. Breathe deeply, but gently.
2. Picture someone you love dearly. See their face. Notice how your heart feels. Envision that it is warm, full, and calm. Imagine a beam of light that encompasses those feelings and send it to the person you love, almost as if you were taking a tiny sun in your hands and shining it on them so that they feel surrounded by warmth, love, comfort, and calm.
3. Next, imagine that same person you love, but now they're in distress. Maybe they're crying or feeling depressed, sick, scared, hungry, or in jeopardy. How does your heart feel now? Full of love and light, yes, but perhaps a different kind of a pull toward the person you love. Maybe it's a kind of an ache. Watch that. Examine it and hold on to it. Now send that beam of light and love and comfort toward your loved one.
4. Next, picture someone you feel ambivalent or neutral about. A coworker or a boss, perhaps? Maybe it's the guy who makes your latte in the morning, or the clerk who finds your clothes on the conveyor belt at the dry cleaners. The school crossing guard. Or the woman who collects your ticket at the mall parking garage.

---

1 The compassion meditation I've included here is based on one created by the Center for Healthy Minds at the University of Wisconsin, Madison, and its researcher Dr. Helen Weng. You can hear an audio guided compassion meditation and read along with its script online at http://ggia.berkeley.edu/practice/compassion_meditation.

Picture that person. See how your heart feels. And then aim your beam of light and love at that person.

5. Next, picture someone you don't like—someone who's hurt or disappointed you or someone you love. Maybe it's an ex-lover or a politician. Maybe it's the neighbor who lets her dog poop in your front yard and never, ever bothers to clean up after her pet. Picture him or her or them clearly, and sit with their image in your mind. Now check in with your heart. How does it feel? Less full? Less warm and full of love? Don't judge it. Just examine how it feels. Do you want that person or persons to suffer? Or do you want to end their suffering? Take that beam of light, love, warmth, comfort, and compassion and aim it at that person or persons. Send the same positive, healing energy you've sent to all of the other people, including yourself.
6. As the meditation ends, send compassion (in that beam of light you hold in your hands, heart, and mind) to all sentient beings in the world. Send out healing and love, comfort and compassion.
7. You've finished the meditation. Continue to sit for a minute or two, breathing calmly and deeply. Open your eyes. Come back to the here and now. And continue on with your day.

HOW I BREATHE

Breathing exercises are so important to do on a daily basis when you are grieving. They helped me deepen my connection with my body and bring awareness to the present moment. I found that when tension in my body was released, my mind was able to take a break from worrying about my loss and how I would cope in the future, which is a side effect of grief.

My grief settles in my belly and chest. I find myself tensing up to protect myself from future pain. Learning to breathe and soften my stomach and chest muscles has helped me to relax and let go of tension.

After completing my body scan meditation, which I do morning and evening, I often ask myself, "What does my breath tell me about how my body is coping with my grief?" When I invite my body to relax, it not only stops my stress reaction, (fight or flight), it reverses the harmful physical effects of stress. My breathing helps me experience a greater sense of calm and control that is essential in my grieving process. I have learned to breathe through my grief and beyond.

Body Scan Meditation (Progressive Relaxation)

Lie on your back in a relaxed position, arms down at your side, palms up. Take a deep breath through your nose, bringing your awareness fully to the present moment. Exhale through your mouth and feel your body relax.

Continue to breathe slowly and gently as you bring your awareness to the top of your head. As the feeling of relaxation begins to spread down from the top of your scalp, feel the muscles in your forehead and temples relax. Allow your eye muscles to relax and your jaw to soften. Let your ears, nose, chin, teeth, and gums relax

Let your cheeks and your jaw soften and let go of all your teaching. Now let the same feeling travel down into your neck. Feel it loosening every muscle and every fiber. With each breath you take, this relaxing feeling becomes deeper and warmer. Feel it work its way down deep into the muscles in your shoulders. Feel it loosen the muscles in your upper arms, your forearms, your hands, relaxing and soothing all the way down to the tips of your fingers.

As your body relaxes so does your mind, and your thoughts become lighter and seem to diminish. You are thinking yourself into a dreamlike state of stillness and relaxation.

Bring your awareness now to your chest and your stomach. Feel these areas gently rise and fall as you breathe. The peaceful sensation is soothing every muscle and relaxing every organ.

Turn your attention to your upper back, and feel this relaxing sensation flow all the way down your spine. Allow it to gradually work its way down your body feeling every muscle in your back relax and unwind. Your entire upper body now has become loose and relaxed.

Now allow this sensation to travel to your hips and start to work its way through your lower body. Relax your glutes, the back of your thighs, the front of your thighs. Feel all these large muscle groups becoming more relaxed and loosening with each passing breath.

Send the same soothing feelings of relaxation down through your knees, and into your calves, ankles, and feet. Allow your entire lower body to relax, allowing any tension from anywhere in your body to flow out to the tips of your toes.

Enjoy your peaceful and relaxed state. Leave the external world behind, and go on an inner journey. A journey to a greater inner peace. Spend as long as you like in this peaceful state visualizing your personal goal and following your highest path. Visualize yourself living your ideal in the personal growth area of your life.

When you are ready to return to your full waking state, take the sense of newfound freedom with you into your daily life. Become aware of your physical body and your surroundings. Wiggle your toes and fingers and when you are ready, in your own time, open your eyes.

Chapter Fourteen

Think

"Whether you think you can, or you think you can't, you're right."
—Henry Ford

True healing from your pain and moving forward in gratitude has a key ingredient: honesty. Being open and honest with yourself and seeing the whole picture of what has happened are absolutely essential to moving through your grief. Being honest hinges first and foremost on how and what you think.

Death is a natural part of the cycle of life. Avoiding thinking about it will *not* empower you and move you toward healing.

Your thoughts create your feelings, not the other way around. When you deliberately change the way you think to focus on the positive rather than the negative, you will speed up your healing process.

But you must also be careful of equating positive thinking with positive-only thinking. Attempting to block out or avoid all negativity isn't healthy or honest, and ultimately will be counterproductive when you're grieving.

Remember your loved one as he or she was—the positive *and* the negative. Do not create an idealized version of their memory. They were complicated, messy, frustrating, lovable, maddening, faulted, and wildly imperfect. I know this because all of us are all of these things.

Remembering only the good, happy, positive things dishonors them and changes your most authentic connections to them. They deserve to be loved and remembered just as they were. The more honest you can be about your memories of them, the easier you will heal from your grief.

While you are grieving, *don't* block any memories of your loved one. This is especially important if they died of a long-term illness. Positive-only thinkers tend to block out the illness and the suffering and perhaps even the death itself. How they died is a part of their life story. Attempting to block it from your memory is unhealthy. All lives deserve to be recognized and honored no matter how they ended. It is possible to find beauty and meaning in illness, suffering, and death.

So if you are focusing only on the positive as an avoidance technique, start to reexamine and recalibrate your whole approach to grieving. You can try to hide from the negative by stuffing the darkness and pain down deep inside you, but it will always find its way out. Don't avoid the lessons life is trying to teach you.

While dealing with a traumatic loss, you may experience sudden temporary upsurges of grief (STUG). They can happen even years after a tragic event, death, or other loss when something triggers memories that cause grief to intensify. Even when the loss has been dormant or is under control, triggers can make the grief resurface and spike.

Triggers usually fall into two categories: *internal* and *external.*

Internal triggers are things you experience inside your mind and body, such as thoughts, memories, emotions, and physical sensations including a racing heartbeat, sweaty palms, or a queasy stomach. Sadness, feelings of abandonment, vulnerability, rage, anger, despair, nervousness, and anxiety are examples of internal triggers.

External triggers are situations, people, or places you might encounter throughout the day. An external trigger could be having or listening to an argument, watching a news report, or witnessing a car accident. It could also be an anniversary, birthday or holiday, seeing a particular person in a particular place, or hearing a song that's connected to a particular memory or person. Certain smells can also trigger memories.

HOW TO THINK

- **Identify your triggers**. Identifying your triggers will help you manage them. Grab a pen and paper. Write down as many internal and external triggers as you can. Ask yourself where you were or what was happening when you experienced the triggers. What did you hear or see? How were you feeling? What were you thinking? What did your body feel like?
- **Remember your triggers—always be aware of them.** Increased awareness about your triggers will make your emotional reactions feel more manageable, easier to understand, valid, and predictable. You will feel more in control, which will positively affect your mood and overall well-being.
- **Don't punish or judge yourself for responding to a trigger.** Allow it to happen. Allow yourself to feel it. And then *let it go.*
- **Try playing the "Yes, but" game.** Let your negative thoughts flow, and follow them with a statement of something good

that came from it. For example, you are thinking of how much you miss your loved one and how sad that makes you. Follow that thought with, *Yes, I miss him, but I loved the time we spent together and I am so grateful for that. He made me laugh, cry, and appreciate the small things in life.* Practice this whenever the negative thoughts arise. Soon it will become a habit, and you will be amazed at how much better you will feel!

- **Recognize the important of self-talk.** Dan Baker, author of *What Happy People Know*, talks about the importance of self-talk and how tuning into it can teach you a lot about yourself. When you are stuck in fear, you are fixated on negative self-talk and your conversations become full of *can't*, *don't*, *shouldn't*, and *won't*. Positive self-talk results in language such as *one possibility is … It would be good to … Thank you for … I appreciate the … The best part is … It's okay to … The good news is … It's my responsibility to ….* Just as changing your life can change your language, changing your language can change your life! Something as simple as thinking of an unexpected situation as a possibility instead of a problem can change the way you look at it. This is also true in grief. Your perception of what has happened and your thought processes are a choice. Start by thinking of the healthy version of your story. Tell yourself all the good things that resulted from the relationship with your loved one. The positive self-talk will make you feel more appreciative and put you back on the road to happiness.

HOW I THINK

Two weeks after Bill's death, I believed I had no choice but to find another home to live. From the home we shared, I can see the train tracks where Bill died and I'm close enough that I can identify the whistle that blows at the exact place on the tracks where his life ended.

The building immediately to the left of our home is the restaurant where we were married. The building to the immediate right of our home is the restaurant where I held Bill's memorial. And across the street is the condominium where Bill and I lived when we were happiest.

How could I continue living amidst all these visual, visceral reminders of Bill, our life together, and his death? I couldn't fathom it.

But if I moved away, what would that accomplish? Even if I left the country or lived alone in a cave, there was no guarantee that I wouldn't encounter something else that would remind me of Bill and bring all of the grief and overwhelming memories and emotions back.

I needed to face each and every one of my triggers, learn how to deal with them, and put them behind me as much as I could. Instead of allowing the train whistles to haunt me, I choose to hear them as almost sacred reminders of the man I loved.

Rather than looking at the restaurant where we were married and allowing sadness to overwhelm memories of our wedding day, I remember the smiles on the faces of our family and friends while we exchanged our vows, as we danced, and celebrated one of the best days of our lives.

When I look at the restaurant where we held Bill's memorial, rather than remembering the grief of that day I choose to focus on the beautiful service where everyone who loved him gathered to honor him and his life.

I know I have a choice about how I respond to constant reminders of Bill. For the first six months after his suicide, every time I saw a black-and-white Toyota FJ Cruiser, I expected to see my husband sitting behind the steering wheel. I even read the license plate to confirm my hope. My heart would race, thinking and dreaming it was him. Over time, I learned to stay in the present. I calmly chose to interpret each sighting of a Cruiser as a reminder of the great adventures we used to have exploring the Mexican countryside together in one.

Even as deliberate and diligent as I've been about identifying my triggers, it's impossible to prepare for all of them. Recently I had a day filled with unexpected and unavoidable triggers. In the morning, as I was pulling on socks to go for a run, I realized they were really big. They weren't my socks. They were Bill's. My initial and instantaneous reaction was sadness, but I quickly recognized it as a trigger moment and stopped myself from going down the rabbit hole of grief. I decided that I would wear Bill's too-big-for-me socks and that they would help me have a strong, empowered run.

Then I went to the mailbox. Inside was a letter addressed to Bill. The postal carrier had written "deceased" in black marker across his name. My heart sank. Then I reminded myself that Bill *is* deceased. The postal carrier was just doing her job, trying to ensure the letter arrived at its intended destination. That is the reality. And that's okay.

Sometimes friends or clients will use the phrase, "I feel as if I've been hit by a train," or "She's such a train wreck" without thinking about what those seemingly harmless words might mean to me. I know they don't mean to be callous or unkind. With that in mind, I've learned not to react.

I make it a priority to practice the *"Yes, but"* game on a daily basis. I don't try to stop my negative thoughts. I let them happen, then let them go. I immediately turn my negative thoughts into positive ones by looking at an alternative way to think.

My most reoccurring thoughts stemmed from my own guilt about not getting Bill the help he needed. *If only I had taken Bill to someone who knew what kind of treatment he needed, he'd still be alive today.* I'd add, **Yes, but** *I didn't know what that treatment consisted of and I did the best I could with what I knew at the time. I am not responsible for his death. He made his own choices in life. I am grateful for the time we spent together and the life lessons I have learned.* My painful memories are my greatest motivators and my biggest source of wisdom.

I've also become accustomed to begin every day with my morning mantra of thought anchors. I repeat them before I leave the house, and even think them throughout the day (especially on extra-challenging days). I'll admit that some days I say them with enthusiasm and vigor while other days I'm just repeating them—but I always say them. And sure enough, I've witnessed them materialize in my life! Below are some of my favorites:

1. It's healthy to grieve.
2. I will give my loss my full attention. I will not run from the pain.
3. I choose to feel better today. I harbor no regrets.
4. I will practice self-care as I heal from my loss.
5. I find new strengths in myself every day.
6. God is helping me heal every day.
7. I am courageous and have the tenacity and ability to envision a bright future for myself.
8. I am open to being happy again.
9. My relationship with my loved one will always be a part of me that I will cherish.
10. My loved one lives on in my thoughts, words, and actions.
11. I will honor my loved one through my renewed determination to enjoy life more fully.
12. I will find peace in all my relationships and situations around me.
13. I will refrain from doing anything that overwhelms me.
14. I have an attitude of gratitude.
15. I will focus on how my loved one lived, not on how they died.
16. I will focus on all the blessings in my life, the people I love, the happiness they bring me, and the positive goals I have set for myself.

17. I have no deadlines on my grieving, and I will not postpone my happiness.
18. Today I have abandoned my old habits and taken up new or positive ones.
19. My body is healthy, my mind is sharp, and my soul is tranquil.
20. My ability to conquer my challenges is limitless; my potential to succeed is infinite. I am blessed with incredible family and friends.

Chapter Fifteen

Talk

"There are many ways of getting strong, sometimes talking is the best way."

—Andre Agassi

It is much easier for grief to overwhelm you when you are out of touch with others. Telling someone how you feel is a vital first step in breaking this isolation so that you can build a network of support. In this chapter, I use the term "talk therapy" to refer to sessions in which talking out loud to another person or persons is a form of working through problems and resolving issues to help you heal.

Many of us find that talking to a friend, family member, mentor, or other confidante in times of trouble or distress is a natural and helpful thing to do. But sometimes they aren't helpful. When this is the case, you may end up feeling even more upset, confused by their advice, or even frustrated and disappointed by their lack of empathy. This can strain relationships, making matters even worse.

Turning to a professional therapist in times of loss, grief, depression, or other kinds of distress is the smart and healthy thing to do—the same as making an appointment to see a doctor if you break your arm. You wouldn't expect your friends or family alone to be able to help you fix your broken arm, would you?

Talk therapy can be a very effective way to deal with negative thoughts and to resolve issues that otherwise might get stuck in a revolving thought cycle in your mind. It can open your imagination to new ways of looking at problems, while reassuring you that you are not alone as you move through the grieving process.

It can also allow you to unburden yourself and ease isolation. Getting things off your chest in a confidential setting can provide you with a great deal of relief, and being honest and connecting with an expert helps to counter the isolating effects of grief. Moreover, that expert can help you gain perspective by helping you make sense of your thoughts or fears. As you talk, you will start to develop understanding and strategies for tackling your grief.

HOW TO TALK

Talk therapy can include one-on-one counseling, grief therapy, family therapy, group counseling, art therapy, music therapy, and support groups led by a professional facilitator. Many of these forms of counseling help a distressed person get through the first weeks, months, and sometimes years of a difficult situation while adjusting to a new life, and can be hugely comforting.

In some instances, people continue to attend these groups to help others navigate issues and situations they have experienced. It may take visiting more than one group or counselor to find one that resonates with your expectations, personality, and style.

Don't give up if the first counselor or group you encounter isn't the right fit for you. The first few visits are like a first date or an interview—they can be awkward and uncomfortable. If you don't feel a connection after the first few visits, move on, but don't throw in the towel on talk therapy altogether. The next therapist or group you meet might be just the right one to bring you the comfort, help, and healing you seek.

Talking things out is a powerful and soothing therapy for almost everyone. Listening to other people talking about what they are going through helps too. It's good to know that you're being heard and that you aren't the only one struggling. It's always nice to know you have something to contribute that might provide insight or comfort to someone else in pain or distress.

You don't need a doctor or anyone else to tell you that you need therapy. If you think talk therapy would be helpful, take the first steps yourself. Find a therapist, counselor, or group in your area by doing an Internet search, asking your medical doctor for a referral, or asking your house of worship, community center, or trusted friends for recommendations.

Talk therapy can help you explore what's going on in your head and move past thought and behavioral patterns that are causing you negative feelings. You may have to face your fears and be honest with yourself, and that can be difficult. You most likely will have "homework" to do between counseling sessions—you may have to recall difficult memories or discuss intimate subjects. But in the end, you should come out feeling better, healthier, and stronger than you were before.

Although many of our issues are universal and can be addressed in group settings, occasionally a serious mental illness or disorder may develop, such as severe depression, panic or eating disorders, and self-harming or manic behavior, and these should be treated by a licensed psychologist or psychiatrist. These healthcare professionals may use forms of talk therapy to treat their patients' more acute mental health issues. Counselors and group facilitators are trained to recognize people who need more serious treatment or interventions and can make recommendations for psychologists and psychiatrists. The types of talk therapy below will help you decide where to start your search for the right counselor or therapist.

Types of Talk Therapy

- **Cognitive Behavioral Therapy (CBT)** is one of the most common types of therapy for grief. In CBT, you look at your thought patterns to see how they can be replaced with more positive ones. Your therapist may ask you to write down your negative thoughts and look for patterns. The therapist and patient work together to identify the behaviors the patient wants to change and then come up with an action plan to do so.
- **Interpersonal therapy (IPT)** is another common type of therapy for grief. IPT focuses on improving your relationship with others and on four main personal challenges: grief over loss, interpersonal disputes, role transitions, and interpersonal skill deficits. Your therapist can teach you new ways to look at your personal relationships and to be more aware of how your actions affect them.
- **Psychodynamic therapy** is not used as often as CBT and IPT for grief, but it may be helpful for some people. In psychodynamic therapy, you reflect on how your past thoughts and actions affect your present life. It also looks at which patterns in your thoughts or actions may cause problems for you, such as ways you might sabotage your own success and healing. Your therapist may also focus on improving your relationships with others as a way to help you manage your grief.

- **Psychoeducation** helps you understand how your grief may lead to depression, its symptoms, and how to treat it. Learning about depression can help you know if your symptoms are getting worse so you can get help early.
- **Support groups** allow you to share your problems and concerns with others who are struggling with the same or similar things. It is useful for those who want to work through their issues in the company of others. The group setting offers unique opportunities to learn from others and get feedback, and it tends to be cheaper than seeing a therapist privately.

HOW I TALK

I found a counselor who had experienced a tragedy similar to mine. I felt confident that she could relate to my pain. That was more important to me than finding a therapist with a PhD who looked to textbooks for answers but had no firsthand experience with grief.

Talk therapy allowed me to face my fears, anger, and resentment, and to understand why I felt so depressed. The counselor assigned me affirmations as part of my therapy, and even though I didn't believe in them at first, they did change my attitude over time. She encouraged me to write, meditate, practice deep breathing, and be particularly mindful of my physical health.

If the brain does not change, there will be no change in behavior or emotion. Verbalizing my fears and anxieties had an actual, physical effect on my brain.

Talk therapy helped me make sense of my feelings and put them into words. Finding a nonjudgmental, empathetic therapist helped me ease the pain of my loneliness, depression, anger, and hurt, and to move forward along my healing journey.

My sessions allowed me to feel authentic. As I progressed, I shed fewer tears and eventually left feeling energized rather than exhausted.

I felt fortunate to have one hour a week set aside for talk therapy to replenish me.

All these years after Bill's death, talk therapy is still an important part of my journey. I'm trained and certified as a grief counselor myself. Regularly, I speak to groups about tools for navigating grief as well as have a growing practice of grief clients whom I see one-on-one.

For me, talk therapy is a gift. I feel grateful and honored to be able to share that gift with others.

Chapter Sixteen

Write

"I write because I don't know what I think until I read what I say."
—Flannery O'Conner

Writing is a wonderfully effective way to navigate through the emotional and physical pain of grief. Sometimes called *writing therapy*, this kind of expressive writing is the simple act of writing down your thoughts, feelings, and observations about traumatic or stressful experiences.

You can write daily or whenever you get the urge. You can write with a pencil, on your laptop, with a magic marker, in a diary, or on the back of a menu. How you do it is entirely up to you. There are no rules, no right or wrong.

Expressive writing has a positive effect on physical and emotional well-being. Writing about stressful events helps you come to terms with them, which reduces the impact of stressors on your physical health. Writing engages your left brain, which is analytical and rational, so while your left brain is occupied, your right brain is free to create and feel.

Most importantly, writing lets you use all of your brainpower to better understand yourself, others, and what is going on in the world around you. This helps reduce anxiety and stress. You're more likely to feel calmer about your feelings, stay in the present, and ultimately release them even if it's just a little at a time. By writing down your feelings and experiences, you can look back on them over time and see what progress you've made—emotionally, spiritually, and otherwise—along the way.

Lest you think this kind of writing exercise is just a bunch of touchy-feely woo-woo self-help nonsense, there is a wealth of scientific research to back it up.

Dr. James W. Pennebaker, chair of the Department of Psychology at the University of Texas at Austin, has studied expressive writing for decades. Time and again he has said that short-term, focused writing has a beneficial effect on everyone, from those dealing with a terminal illness to victims of violent crime to college students facing freshman-year transitions.

"When people are given the opportunity to write about emotional upheavals, they often experience improved health," Pennebaker says. "They go to the doctor less. They have changes in immune function."

In one study, Pennebaker asked forty-six healthy college students to write about either personally traumatic events or trivial topics for fifteen minutes on four consecutive days. For six months after the experiment's conclusion, students who had written about traumatic events reported visiting the campus health center less frequently and even used pain relievers less often than those who had written about inconsequential matters.

"People who engage in expressive writing report feeling happier and less negative than before writing," Pennebaker wrote in his book *Writing to Heal.* "Similarly, reports of depressive symptoms, rumination, and general anxiety tend to drop in the weeks and months after writing about emotional upheavals."

In his studies, Pennebaker gave participants the following basic instructions and assignment:

> *"Over the next four days, write about your deepest emotions and thoughts about the emotional upheaval that has been influencing your life the most. In your writing, really let go and explore the event and how it has affected you. You might tie this experience to your childhood, to your relationship with your parents, people you have loved or love now, or even your career. Write continuously for twenty minutes."*

Pennebaker tells the story of a young woman he worked with who had lost her husband in an accident. The woman's colleagues in graduate school had praised her for her courage in the face of her spouse's sudden death and for how "smoothly" she had handled his death. She came to Pennebaker because she felt she needed to write about her loss. By the fourth day of writing, she said she had been transformed. Within two months of the expressive writing assignment, the woman had quit graduate school and moved back to her hometown. The writing experience had made her realize she was on a life path she no longer wanted and that she had been putting on a false, cheerful front with her friends.

"As a researcher, I could say, 'Well here I have a technique that made an individual drop out of school, stop pursuing an advanced degree and return home,' " Pennebaker says. "It was a dramatic change, and it sounds like a failure. But from her perspective, it wasn't."

In fact, the woman felt that those four days of writing saved her life.

HOW TO WRITE

- Find a time and a place where you won't be disturbed by anyone else.
- Write uninterrupted for at least ten to twenty minutes every day.
- Don't worry about spelling, grammar, or structure.
- Write only for yourself.
- Write about something extremely personal, important, painful, or traumatic to you.
- Deal only with feelings and situations you can handle right now.
- Don't judge what you write. Just express it. Simply write it down.
- Write quickly. This frees your brain from all the guilt or any other negative blocks you may be experiencing. Soon you'll discover that your writing has become a nonjudgmental friend. Writing also is the cheapest form of therapy you can find. Bonus!

HOW I WRITE

Initially I was not on board with the concept of writing as therapy. It just seemed too easy—so basic an idea that the benefits would be minimal. I didn't believe it could have any healing effect on me. I was wrong.

After much coaxing from my therapist, I decided the least I could do was reach out to Bill after his death by writing him a letter on Valentine's Day. Tears streamed down my face while I wrote.

One year later, I wrote again to Bill on Valentine's Day. When I go back and read my letters, I realize just how far I've come on my journey through grief. Writing has become an instrumental part of my healing, and it will be for you too.

Write yourself through grief and into a new world of light, health, and new beginnings. You can write yourself well, and it won't cost you anything!

February 14 2013

Hi Bill,

It's Valentine's Day today. I'm having a really rough time—I really miss you! You always gave me a single red rose and always would replace it when it died. I bought a red rose today like you would have done for me. Thank you!

I know you didn't mean to hurt me and everyone else that loved you. I am so sorry I didn't take your suicide threats seriously. I never dreamed you would hurt yourself. You worked too hard on your physique, I couldn't imagine you destroying it. I don't know what made you hate yourself so much.

You were such a special man, so loving, and I guess, so lost.

Your memorial was beautiful. It was right next door at the Chart House. I saw you there. We all did. The monarch butterfly that flew in front of your picture was amazing. Mom wrote a verse for the back of your memorial card. It had a monarch butterfly above it. Your picture was on the front. I sent the large canvas photo of you and the extra cards to your dad. He arranged a small service in Houston for you. Your mom didn't come as it was too hard for her.

I know you didn't want to end up in Texas but your dad wanted you buried between your grandparents. They idolized you. Your parents recently bought their plots there, too, so you all will be together.

Did you see Smoke and I cuddled together at night? I know you never thought I was seeing someone else. I know you had already made a plan and were trying to push me away.

Thank you for not taking all the money out of our bank account that morning. I found the envelope and note addressed to your father. What made you change your mind? It would have been really hard to start over with nothing.

Your parents could not accept that you killed yourself. I let them believe it was an accident, thinking it might be easier for them. Your dad emails me every week. He is blaming himself. He said he should have flown into Orange County, that if he had this would not have happened.

Did you realize he was on the train you ran in front of?

I listen to the train whistles all day and night. I pretend it's you signaling me that you are at peace. Most of the time, though, it doesn't work. My usual thought is of you being struck by a 1,000-ton train. Why did you choose that? Why so violent? That is what makes this so hard.

I hope your soul left your body before impact. I hope you didn't feel any pain. I don't know for sure.

I visited Pastor James at Saddleback and on the way I had to stop at the red light for the train to pass. That was beyond heart-stopping for me. What happened when you were struck? Where are your earring and cell phone? I didn't get them in your personal stuff. That was Grandma's diamond earring. I saw your cell phone on the tracks in a photo in the paper. Oh well …

I've wondered how you would be doing now if I had killed myself and what you would be doing to heal. Would you have survived this? I don't know. Sometimes I think when people go through a divorce and have their hearts ripped out it's even worse. Their loved one is alive, yet they are estranged. I don't know what to do or say to help your parents with their pain. They are "crying inside"—that's what your dad said.

I hope you don't mind me using your story to help others. I need to help others. I need to do something. I refuse to let this happen to someone else. I spoke at Saddleback College and a local high school about depression, steroids, and benzos.

I know if you had to do it all over again you would have chosen a different path for your life. I looked up two of your old buddies from your bodybuilding days. Both are divorced and not doing well physically. What a ridiculous sport. I'd like to have it abolished. Your friend Lou is expected to die any day. He spoke at your memorial. I'll go to his memorial for you. Watch for him …

I hope I made your life a little better while you were here. I'm trying to understand your pain so I can be relieved you are at peace. I still feel I should have done more.

I'll see you again, okay? Don't forget me …

I love you,

Kristi

February 14, 2014

Hi Bill,

This is my second Valentine's Day without you. I know you are at peace and looking out for me. I have stopped trying to figure out the why's and what-if's, and am letting go of my guilt. I learned over this past year just to accept you and your decision for what it was: ***your*** *decision.*

I believe you had multiple things going on at once and you were so ill that suicide seemed like a rational solution to end your pain. Years of steroid abuse, benzo withdrawal, and genetics all were there to create the perfect storm.

I believe we spent the perfect amount of time together and even though I didn't get to say goodbye, I say hello to you every day. I feel so badly that you were suffering and so alone. I know you are not suffering now. That gives me peace.

I am trying to share my experience with others and help them with their journeys through grief. Most of my clients are moms whose sons have died by drug overdoses or suicide. It breaks my heart to hear their stories, but I'm not afraid of their pain, as I've been there. I am not the only one that has been down that path.

I have developed strength, compassion, and I have a completely different perspective on life now.

I recently organized my office and went through all the files of research I'd done over the past two years looking for answers. Article after article about steroid abuse, depression, suicide, anxiety, side effects of Benzodiazepines. It was an endless search and I know everyone I meet will go through this process, too. It's long and exhausting, but a necessary step in their healing.

I have been working hard not to let my experiences over the past two years control my life and become consumed by the pain. I dissected every part of what happened and have exhausted it to the point of letting it all go. I don't cringe when I hear the train whistles blowing all day. Trains still will carry passengers and will not stop to accommodate me.

I know I have a greater purpose in life and I am struggling to find it. I will be okay and I hope again to find happiness. I'm more impatient with people and their pettiness, but try hard not to respond harshly or negatively, as they are in a different place than I am and that's not all bad.

I have been somewhat lonely lately, so thoughts of you make me smile. I would give anything to hold your hand one more time. It's the little things I miss the most.

You know my strengths and I will continue to make a difference in the lives of others. I already have in small ways, but that is not enough.

Smoke turned twenty last month. She looks in the corner of the bedroom every morning and lets out an outrageously loud howl. I think she sees you there.

Love,

Kristi

Chapter Seventeen

Trust

"It doesn't matter if a million people tell you what you can't do, or if ten million tell you no. If you get one yes from God that's all you need."
—Tyler Perry

It is possible to navigate the stormy seas of grief without any kind of faith or belief in a higher power. People have done it for thousands of years and will continue to do so. But for the life of me, I have no idea how they do it.

Faith is central to my life—never more so than when I'm faced with grief. I'm Christian, but you don't need to believe the same things I do to make it through grief. However, I do believe spiritual engagement with something greater than yourself is necessary to help you move through your grief.

Words such as "religion," "faith," "believe," and even "God" are tough for some people to wrap our hearts and minds around. These words can even be unhelpful emotional triggers. But in this chapter, let's put all of these spiritual words and ideas under an umbrella and call it *trust*. Feel free to substitute whatever spiritual word or words that are authentic for you in place of *trust*.

Death forces you to confront the spiritual questions you may have been avoiding or haven't taken the time to figure out. Who am I? Why am I here? Where am I going? Trust plays a big part in the grief process. Like any other tool for self-care, try to use your trust in a healthy, appropriate way.

We mourn life's losses from the inside out. It is only when we are spiritually nurtured that we find the courage to mourn openly and honestly. To practice spiritual self-care means you are allowing yourself to have the courage to pay attention to your needs. It's in spiritually nurturing yourself, and allowing yourself the time and attention you need to journey through your grief, that you will find meaning, purpose, and perhaps even joy.

Spirituality—what or whom you trust—influences your fundamental views of life and reassures you that you are not alone and that, however difficult life may be right now, many before you have walked the path you are on.

Your grief journey is not a dead-end; it's a well-marked trail. Trust is a source of strength and support. Also, it can be a powerful antidote for the loneliness that accompanies any loss. Trust can and will take many forms as you seek peace, comfort, and clarity at this critical time in your life. Try to be open to it in whatever form it takes. What trust cannot do is immunize you from the pain of grief or give you back your loved one.

It can't provide you with a shortcut through the grieving process, but it will certainly accompany you on your journey.

Grief can shake our beliefs about and connection with God (a word I'm using to represent a higher power). The whole concept of God can be difficult to grasp in the midst of your grief, and it may be difficult to find any serenity in your beliefs.

Anger—at God, at the universe, even at the person who's died—may be part of why you're questioning your faith. Why would a just, loving God allow this to happen? If your God was present in a physical form, you probably wouldn't have much to say to him right now.

First of all, please know that yes, you can be angry at God. It's natural and it's okay. Be honest with God. Yell and scream at God if you feel like. I did. I'm happy to report no thunderbolt sightings, and I wasn't turned to stone or a pillar of salt. Trust me, God can take it.

A passage in the Bible says whoever seeks God will find God. So in these times of grief, reach out in whatever way you can to a higher power. Ask for peace and solace. You can even ask for joy. All of these things are gifts from God. If we ask for them, we'll get them. They might not arrive how and when we expect or wish them to, but if you ask—if you seek them—you will find them.

HOW TO TRUST

- Accept that life is not fair. It is harsh and stressful, but it can also be beautiful and meaningful. Some people have it easier than others, and some get the short end of the stick so badly that you can't even bear to imagine yourself in their shoes. Concede that life is unfair, but know that there is still so much to be grateful for.
- Don't ask *why* or *why me*? Instead, ask *how* and *what can I learn from this*?

- Search for spiritual meaning at your own pace. Allow yourself time to process all that has happened.
- Be kind to yourself and others and allow your grief process to unfold naturally.
- Acknowledge the signs no matter how big or small every day. (My husband's favorite bird was the hummingbird. Whenever I see hummingbirds, I like to think it's his way of letting me know he's watching over me.)
- Create new rituals. Rituals affirm landmarks in our lives.
- Recognize that new beliefs can grow from your grief into a deeper, more mature understanding of the divine dimensions of life.

HOW I TRUST

As I've mentioned, my personal spiritual beliefs are Christian ones. During my childhood and adolescence, life revolved entirely around family, farming, and our church, Trinity Lutheran. We went to Sunday school, rarely missed a Sunday church service, sang in the choir, took confirmation classes, and were confirmed. We prayed. We stuck to the Golden Rule. We were good, hard-working people. We were good neighbors.

My faith was simple but strong: Do unto others as you would have them do unto you. Be kind. Be honest. Don't be selfish. Don't be greedy. Make do with what you have. Don't complain.

When I left the farm and headed to college at a Lutheran university in Minneapolis, theology classes were part of our required studies. Rather than deepen or expand my faith, theology made God and faith feel complicated.

But I never lost faith. It was always there, just more in the background than it is now especially in Bill's absence.

For the last several years, I've attended Saddleback Church in Lake Forest, California. It has campuses throughout Orange County and abroad. It was founded in 1980 by Pastor Rick Warren and his wife, Kay. Rick Warren's book *The Purpose Driven Life* was one of the few books—if not the only book—Bill actually read from cover to cover. He kept it on his nightstand and took it outside with him to relax every afternoon, slowly digesting every page. Bill found so much inspiration and solace in reading *The Purpose Driven Life* that he sent his father a copy. It was one of the few books, if not the only book, that I know Bill Sr. read as well.

When Bill was at his worst and his anxiety was out of control, the only counselor who got through to him was Ginny, a volunteer at Saddleback's Rancho Capistrano campus. Ginny was amazingly compassionate. During one of her sessions with us, she got down on her knees, held Bill's shaking hands, and asked him to pray with her. Tears streamed down Bill's face as he professed his faith and she prayed for his healing.

Bill loved to attend the services at Saddleback Rancho Capistrano as the pastor there, James Valencia, made us feel so special and loved. We were part of an amazing church family.

Six months after Bill died, Rick and Kay Warren's youngest son, Matthew, took his own life after years of struggling with mental illness. Matthew's suicide sent ripples of shock and grief through the Saddleback community and beyond. Thankfully, the Warrens didn't try to hide what had happened or why. Instead, they became even more vocal about the importance of mental health care and the role that the church had to play in fighting the social stigma of mental illness and in making sure that people who need help get it.

The summer after Matthew Warren's death, after taking a sixteen-week sabbatical to mourn and grieve privately, the Warrens returned to the pulpit at Saddleback Church and launched an eight-**part sermon** series called "How to Get Through What You're Going Through."[2] It helped me find hope and peace during the most painful and trying periods of my life. It was as if Pastor Rick and Kay had taken me by the hand and walked me through that proverbial valley of the shadow of death.

It was exactly what I needed to hear, exactly when I needed to hear it. Some people might call that providence. Whatever you want to name it, I call it a blessing. On that first Sunday back in the pulpit, Rick Warren said:

> *What you know is what gets you through. Now I don't like to say this as your pastor because I love you, but you're gonna go through tough times and you, too, will experience major losses in life. There is no growth without change, there is no change without loss, there is no loss without pain, and there is no pain without grief.... Life doesn't make sense but we can still have peace because God is with us and God loves us. You have noticed, I'm sure, that life is often confusing. There are more questions than answers, and there are a lot of unanswered questions. And the truth is we simply don't know why things happen the way they do.*

We're not going to know, not on "this side of eternity." We're not going to have the answers to most of our "why" questions. So stop asking why. It doesn't help.

After Bill died, I got angry with God. I yelled at God. I swore at God. I wanted to know why. Why would God allow Bill to die? What had I done to deserve this kind of pain and sorrow? Why did God

---

2 Pastor Rick Warren's entire "How to Get Through What You're Going Through" sermon series is available free of charge online at https://saddleback.com/watch/media/series/2040/how-to-get-through-what-youre-going-through.

want me to be alone? If God loves me, why would God allow Bill to kill himself?

"God has not promised to give you an explanation for everything that happens in the world," Pastor Rick said in that sermon, "but he has promised that you're not going to go through it alone."

Sorrow is a godly emotion, he said. The Bible says that even God grieves.

"Grieving is a good thing," Pastor Rick said. "Grieving is the way we get through the changes in life."

And then he said something that stuck with me:

> *"God wants to take your greatest pain and turn it into your life message. He wants to use your mess for a message, he wants to use your test as a testimony. The very thing you want least to talk about in your life is the very same thing God wants to use most to help other people. Your ministry comes out of your pain."*

I was standing at a crossroads. I could use my pain to help others—to educate them about mental illness, suicide, and its warning signs; about addiction and recovery; about grieving and how to get through whatever it is you're going through. Or I could remain silent and alone, wallowing in self-pity. To me it was a no-brainer.

I had a purpose. I had a vision. And I even had a mantra.

"Never waste your pain," Pastor Rick preached in his final sermon in the series. "Let God heal it, recycle it—and use it to bless other people."

Never waste your pain.

I promised myself—and God—that I wouldn't.

I'd been a fitness professional for more than twenty years. I had a career, but I don't think I'd had a vocation—a true calling, if you will—until then.

I will never have the answers to all of those "why" questions, but I could in some small way make sense of Bill's death and my grief by transforming it into a way to help others. I started by sharing Bill's story with friends, and then with strangers, and then with a couple of newspaper reporters; in an Internet video; on the radio. I enrolled in a training program to learn how to become a grief counselor and now have a growing practice with clients of all ages whom I help navigate the grieving process. I started speaking publicly about suicide, mental health, and addiction in high schools and junior high schools; to civic and church groups; and most recently in a podcast called *The Grief Girl.*

None of this happened overnight. It evolved slowly, over months and now years. But it started with a leap of faith and something else Rick Warren talked about in that last sermon in his grief series. He said:

> *... to touch other people, you need to be honest—with God, yourself and others—and you need to be vulnerable.*

I learned that to fulfill my purpose and not squander my pain, to be honest about Bill's death and its aftermath, to be open and willing to share what grief has taught me, meant taking risks. I could be hurt again or more or worse. Maybe no one would need or want my help. Perhaps nothing I had to say would be worth hearing. I could fail. I could be rejected.

To heed my calling, I had to be vulnerable. And to do that, I had to **trust**. I had to trust God. I had to trust my family and friends. I had to trust my teachers. I had to trust my clients. I had to trust my instincts. I had to trust my wisdom. I had to trust that still, small voice that says, *You are not alone.*

Navigating grief takes patience with yourself and with others. I've been trying to learn how to trust again by practicing trustworthiness myself. Before Bill's death, I had no idea how much a greeting card could mean to me. Or a phone call. Or an email. Just knowing that someone was thinking of me means the world to me now.

Now when I know someone is grieving or going through a tough time, I try my hardest to show up. I send the card. I make the phone call. I stop by unannounced. I bring food. I do the thing—whatever it is—to let them know they're not alone.

The more I try to cultivate trustworthiness in my own relationships, no matter how casual, the more I am able to trust again.

Chapter Eighteen

Be

"Be passionate. Be courageous. Be your best."
—Gabrielle Giffords

Your loss is now a part of who you are. It is your new normal. But how do you get accustomed to and exist with this new part?

"Being" is all about living in the present with gratitude and without judgment. You must learn to live each day in the present—here and now—and to its fullest. Don't spend another day obsessing over the past or worrying about the future. This will help you to shift your thoughts away from your grief towards an appreciation of the moment and a larger perspective on life.

No one is immune from experiencing heartbreak, loneliness, failure, and loss. Some of us can put negative experiences behind us and move on with hope and optimism. Others can't seem to let difficult times go.

People who can't let go of the past keep replaying the bad times in their minds. They revisit the difficult days in those quiet moments when they are alone and have time to think. They replay painful memories like a broken record. They feel the sadness and relive all the emotions that go with the difficult times for days, weeks, months, and years, never allowing the past and pain to recede from their present reality.

We can choose to stop negative thoughts from replaying and instead focus on the present moment. This is referred to as living in the present or mindfulness. Rather than letting your mind wander to something that happened in the past or might happen in the future, pay attention to what is happening right now.

Where are you? What is the weather like? Are you warm or cold? What do you hear? What do you feel? What do you see? Who are you with? What are they doing? What are they saying?

Stay in control of your thoughts by watching them go by—like a movie or slide show without trying to hold on to them and without judging or assigning value to them.

Don't obsess over your thoughts. See them, and then let them go. Use all your senses to stay in the moment. Notice the lights, shapes, colors, and textures. Just live in this moment right now and realize that right now the past doesn't really matter and the future doesn't either.

Moving forward when you've lost someone doesn't mean that your grief ends or that your relationship is over. Moving forward is a personal decision. Only you can decide what's right for you. Moving forward and letting go doesn't mean forgetting and certainly doesn't signal the end of your grief. It means learning to live a balanced life and transforming your pain into healthy creative outlets.

Get to know your grief in your own way whether it's through your own experiences or those of others close to you. Don't be shy about starting conversations about grief with your loved ones as you all might be able to provide some healing and insight to one another. Grief makes us feel helpless and is something that we cannot do alone.

The need for others exists in all of us even if that need is just to be held while we cry. There is such beauty in the silence of a tearful hug from a friend, relative, or even a stranger. Allow others to see and appreciate your heart and look for the beauty in theirs as well.

Know that grief changes and morphs over time, and that it's important for you to allow yourself to change and morph too.

If you learn to be mindful of your thoughts, your life will begin to change. You will be a new person, unburdened by experiences you can't change or by anxiety for the future.

HOW TO BE

- Develop an attitude of gratitude. Expressing gratitude will increase your overall well-being, from better relationships to health to sleep. Gratitude grows the more you use it.
- Be grateful for whomever and whatever you can. Learn the simple joy of just living.
- Be grateful for the people who show up. There is nothing better than having loved ones in your life.
- Be grateful for your breath. Inhale "help." Exhale "thank you."
- Be grateful for beauty. In your grief, it may be hard to see beauty and it may even be hard to remember it, but it's always there waiting for you to notice it. Eventually, you'll see it again as you move through your grief toward healing and wholeness. It will inspire, amaze, humor, and comfort you. It will give you hope, peace, and even surprise you with joy.
- Be grateful for yourself.

- Be grateful for however far you have come in your journey of grief.
- Be grateful for your patience and self-compassion.

HOW I AM

As the thick fog of shock and despair began to clear, I got outside of myself and tried to help others—instinctively, I knew that this was the best way for me to deal with my grief. I became determined to share the hard-earned lessons I'd learned while navigating through the tunnel of grief.

Every morning I list five positive things that will happen during the day. I say them out loud. This distracts me from veering toward negative thoughts. My life has been affected by my loss, but I am not defined by it. I also think or say thought anchors to myself throughout the day when I have a quick moment for reflection.

My day starts and ends with gratitude. Gratitude is a high-powered flashlight that will cut through grief's darkness and confusion and help you see your way forward. I list all the people and things I'm grateful for. This has become so second-nature to me that I say them even when I'm on autopilot, such as when driving or cleaning.

Once I learned to focus on looking for things to be grateful for, I found that I began to appreciate the simple things that I previously took for granted. Gratitude is not just about getting what I want, but is an all- the -time gratitude, where I looked for the good, even in my grief. I learned to start bringing gratitude to all my life experiences. My attitude of gratitude determines whether I can feel grateful in spite of everything I'm going through. It is a key element in finding happiness. Happiness is a choice, and I choose to be happy.

And every day I try to give something to someone. Once I saw the difference I could make in another person's life, my own problems seemed smaller and helped me see my life in a whole new light. The good feelings I experience when helping others are just as important to my health as exercise and a healthy diet.

It's the little things like the smile on someone's face when I help them with something they couldn't do for themselves, or that thankful person who lets me know I made a difference, that brings me great joy. And that's the greatest feeling in the world.

When you are ready, you will want to try to give something back too. Give to a friend, neighbor, or stranger. Give to your family, your workplace, your community, your world.

None of us can ever know the full extent of our influence on others. What may seem like an inconsequential gesture to you might feel like a miracle to someone else. Volunteer at a local food bank, weed an elderly neighbor's flowerbed, have a garage sale and donate the proceeds to a children's charity. Whatever you do, just know that you are providing comfort and aid.

I know that I've been through a loss, but I haven't lost everything. I can still enjoy the moments that each day brings and make a difference to others. These things in themselves are miracles. A miracle doesn't always have to be a grand action. If you are able to deliver a healthy meal today for someone in need, or get to the gym for the first time since your loss, you've made a miracle happen. Regardless of their size, miracles are extraordinary as long as they are extraordinary to *you*.

Find joy and gratitude in the people and things around you.

Just be...the miracle.

Epilogue

To be human is to know Grief.
It lies in wait, then arrives unexpectedly,
Sparing no one from a visit.

An uninvited guest,
It makes itself at home
Blinding and overwhelming me.

I turn from it, refusing to acknowledge it.
I see others wildly railing against it.
But in time it's no longer my enemy.

I learn to live with it
Discovering it's my greatest teacher,
Gaining compassion for all beings.

Hope comes at last, a welcome visitor.
In due time, her companion Joy appears.
Enlightened, I embrace them all.

Afterword

The following article ran in the March 8, 2014, edition of the Orange County Register *newspaper.*

Suicide by train: Shared tragedies upend string of lives

By Keith Sharon and Greg Hardesty

On the day he died, Bill Brotherton Jr. couldn't find anything for breakfast. Usually, he was a protein guy. Six eggs mixed into a bowl of oatmeal. Microwaved. If he had toast, it didn't have butter.

A body builder and personal trainer since his 20s, Bill Jr. treated his body—a ripped 250 pounds until the last few months of his life—as if he wanted to live forever.

But that morning, Bill Jr., 54, was alone in his Dana Point home overlooking the harbor. A plaque in the living room read: "Your life is happening right now. Make it amazing."

His wife, Kristi Hugstad, had left him the previous night. She'd gone to stay with her sister. She left because for the first time in the seven months he'd been showing signs of mental illness, she was afraid of her husband.

Later that day, Bill Brotherton Jr. ran up a graveled embankment in Capistrano Beach, stood on the train tracks that run near the ocean and looked at the engineer of the northbound 808 Metrolink train—more than 1,000 tons of steel bearing down on him at about 60 mph.

Bill Jr.'s choice altered dozens of lives, from the engineer and conductor on the train, to the passengers they served, to the bystanders who happened to see the carnage.

Nationwide, about 400 people a year commit suicide by train, according to the Federal Railroad Administration.

In Orange County, where nearly 68 miles of track snake through neighborhoods from San Clemente to Anaheim—and where 58 people killed themselves on train tracks from 2002 to 2012— the rate of suicides by train is slightly higher.

And where the train runs from the San Diego County line to Dana Point, where there are few fences and many pedestrians, the deaths are clustered. Since 1986, at least 19 people—including Bill Brotherton Jr.— have died on that six-mile stretch of track.

Bill Jr.'s death devastated people who loved him, his acquaintances—even some people who didn't know him at all.

A close friend, years sober, fell off the wagon.

A witness, a total stranger, sought counseling.

His aging father eventually shut down, not speaking with some relatives and turning off his phone.

And his widow has embarked down a new path.

More than a year later, the ripple effect of Bill Jr.'s final act still runs wide and deep, as it often does when a person chooses suicide by train.

At 5:30 a.m. on Oct. 10, 2012, the day he died, Bill Jr. called his father in Texas.

Bill Brotherton Sr. retired from a successful career in the oil and gas industry. The 80-year-old was planning to spend the rest of his days on his farm, near Houston, raising goats.

"Dad, there is no food in the house," Bill Jr. said. "We used to have enough food for a week. Now, there is nothing."

Bill Jr. sounded helpless.

Bill Sr. was worried.

"My head is scrambled," Bill Jr. told his mother, Bess, when Bill Sr. passed the phone to her.

Bill Sr. quickly put together a plan. He would bring Bill Jr. home to Texas, help him land a new job; get him to a mental health clinic to get his head straight.

He also booked the first flight he could get to Southern California.

It was cheaper to land in San Diego and take the train to Orange County. He had done it many times, and he told Bill Jr. to pick him up at the San Juan Capistrano train station, as usual. He would arrive just after 5 p.m.

Around 7 a.m., Bill Jr. got a text from Aaron Carlow, a longtime friend and workout partner.

"No gym," Aaron wrote, canceling their workout session.

"OK," Bill Jr. texted back.

In recent months, Bill Jr. had battled a muscle pull in his chest, limiting his once herculean weight routine.

"I had to spot him carefully when he did dumbbells," Aaron said. "I could see his strength was fading."

At 9 a.m., Bill Jr. went to the Bank of America in Dana Point.

Kristi later would find an envelope addressed to Bill Sr. with a note that said, "Cashier's check for $65,000," though there was no check inside. She believes Bill Jr. went to the bank that morning intending to withdraw everything they had and send it to his parents in Texas.

No one knows why Bill Jr. never completed the transaction. No money was withdrawn. No mail went to Texas.

As Bill Jr. was walking away from the bank, he bumped into a friend, Debbie Preble, a hairdresser he had dated years earlier.

Debbie noticed that he didn't look like his former self. His once-glowing tan now just made his skin look weathered. His once action-hero muscles sagged.

"What's wrong?" she asked, giving him a hug.

"Preble," he said upon seeing her. He always called her by her last name. "How's your marriage?" she asked.

"Over," he said.

She made small talk about meeting for lunch soon.

Then Bill Jr. walked away.

Every train engineer and conductor refers to something known, simply, as the "number."

It's the number of people their trains have hit while they've been on duty.

Amtrak, which employs the people who run Metrolink trains, declined to allow the engineer and conductor from the train that Bill Jr. stood in front of be interviewed.

But the *Register* was able to talk with an Amtrak engineer and conductor who deal regularly with what is known in the transportation industry as "trespasser strikes."

Both said two things.

First, train suicides are part of the job. There is absolutely nothing an engineer or conductor can do to prevent a train from hitting someone determined to throw themselves in front of one.

Second, every one of those deaths is devastating.

"You never get used to it," said Amtrak Engineer Douglas Busler, 57, who said he stopped counting but estimates his number to be as high as 20, most of them suicides. Busler, railroading for nearly 35 years, almost always was forced to watch the final act from his seat in the front of the train.

At Amtrak, engineers and conductors on trains involved in fatalities are required to take at least three days off. They also are offered psychological counseling.

Conductor Kirk Lewis, 52, who has worked for Amtrak for 20 years, estimates that his number is 17 or 18. When a person is struck, it is the job of the conductor, who usually roams the train and deals with passengers, to call for emergency help and then run outside to help the injured.

Trains are equipped with defibrillators, and conductors are supposed to use them on survivors. But survivors are rare.

"The more incidents you are involved in, the more it affects you," Lewis said.

"It's just as traumatic every time."

Lewis recounted one of the more recent suicides he handled, in July 2012. As he stepped out of the train, he saw horrific carnage and had one thought:

"Five minutes ago, this was a human being."

About 2:30 p.m. on the day he died, Bill Jr. got a phone call from Bill Sr.

The plane had arrived in San Diego, and Bill Sr. asked how his son was doing. "Fine," Bill Jr. said.

But Bill Sr. remained concerned. So after he arrived from the San Diego Airport at the Metrolink station in Oceanside, he called Bill Jr. again.

"(I'm) en route," Bill Sr. said, settling into his seat on the train.

"I'll pick you up in San Juan Capistrano, just like I always have," Bill Jr. said, reassuring his father that everything was fine.

By train, the ride from Oceanside to San Juan Capistrano is 36 minutes.

Bill Jr. and Kristi met through a mutual friend in 2005.

"We were together every day after that," said Kristi, who, in July of that year, became Bill Jr.'s second wife.

At first, they thrived, personally and professionally. Kristi, like Bill Jr., worked as a personal trainer. They pooled their money to buy the Pulse gym in Dana Point. Everything, she said, was going great.

Then, in 2009, the economy tanked.

By October of 2011, Bill Jr. and Kristi were facing financial difficulties. They moved from Dana Point to Rosarito Beach in Mexico. There, they lived on the fifth floor of the Califia Resort condominium complex, a beautiful gym in the basement and the Pacific Ocean just outside their window.

But Bill Jr. was anxious. Kristi said women no longer approached him and asked to touch his muscles. He was getting old.

"He was not being validated," Kristi said. "There was no fan club. He wanted to be noticed. He left his identity in Orange County."

On March 24, 2012, Bill Jr. couldn't sleep. What followed was a four-day break from reality. Kristi said her husband turned mean and began pacing, threatening to throw himself off the balcony.

He sat on the couch and rocked.

Kristi believes his mental problems were exacerbated by decades-long steroid use.

"Something, chemically, went wrong in his brain," Kristi said.

Bill Sr. visited the couple in Rosarito, and he could see his son was hurting.

They talked about Bill Jr. returning to California and getting work as a personal trainer for senior citizens. They talked about Bill Jr. and Kristi moving to Texas. Bill Sr. said he could introduce Bill Jr. to oil men who needed inspectors for their offshore rigs.

After his father left, Bill Jr. told Kristi there was no way he was going to Texas.

In April of 2012, Bill Jr. and Kristi moved back to Dana Point.

Kristi quickly set up Bill Jr. with a carousel of psychologists, psychiatrists and other physicians.

On April 21, Kristi found a note on the kitchen table.

"Baby, you need to move on with your life and find somebody better. I can't do this anymore, Love Bill."

It read, to Kristi, like a suicide note. But Bill Jr. was not dead. He was in the bathroom.

He told her he had tried to kill himself by taking 20 Ambien tablets and drinking half a bottle of Nyquil.

Kristi took him to Mission Hospital in Laguna Beach. He was placed on a 5150 involuntary hold, meaning he would be required to spend the next 72 hours under psychiatric evaluation. He was transferred to a facility in Santa Ana. Without explanation, Bill was discharged in less than 24 hours.

Kristi felt her husband was falling through the cracks in an inadequate mental health system.

On May 27, Bill Jr. disappeared. Kristi called Bill Sr., who, from Texas, filed a missing persons report with the Orange County Sheriff's Department.

But Bill Jr. was only gone for about eight hours. When he came home, his bald head was so badly sunburned Kristi could see blisters. She asked him where he had been.

"Walking next to the train tracks," Bill Jr. said.

On the day he died, Bill Jr. parked his white and black Toyota FJ Cruiser on Coast Highway across the street from the Riviera Resort in Capistrano Beach.

On the train, Bill Sr. thought about what he would say to his son to get him to come back home to Texas.

The Metrolink train, carrying a relatively light load of about 50 passengers, hit a top speed of 90 mph between San Clemente and Capistrano Beach. It was 5 p.m., 63 degrees.

As it passed through Capistrano Beach, the train was in the process of slowing to 45 mph so it could negotiate a right turn as it headed inland, near a bend at mile marker 200.3.

In his White Jeep Cherokee, Chris O'Neill, 57, drove along Coast Highway, scouting the best break for an evening surf.

He heard a train whistle and glanced in its direction.

He saw a large, bald man run up the rocky embankment and stand on the train tracks.

"His arms were stretched to the sides, like Jesus on the cross," Chris said.

The windshield of the Metrolink train is made from Federal Rail Administration-approved 223 glazing safety glass. It is 3/8 of an inch thick, built to protect the engineer from projectiles like rocks, B.B.s and bullets.

And from trespassers.

Bill Brotherton Jr. looked straight through that glass. The train's brakes squealed, kicking up dirt and rocks.

It was 5:10 p.m.

As Chris O'Neill watched a train hit a man his car was showered with rocks and blood.

"I saw a man turn himself into a thousand pieces of gore," he said. "Then I thought, 'Did this really happen?' "

He kept driving, fumbling with his cellphone to dial 911.

Twenty minutes after O'Neill got home, the police called. They said they couldn't find a body. (Eventually, they found a torso about 75 yards from where the train stopped.) Momentarily, O'Neill thought he had imagined the whole thing.

But when he walked outside, he knew he hadn't. His car was covered with debris from the collision. The police had told him to wash it off immediately because it was hazardous material.

As he washed his car, he saw the debris snake down into the street's storm drain. He dried his car and threw the towel away.

Then he rinsed the street.

Over the next few days, O'Neill was unable to sleep. He missed work and started seeing a psychologist.

Just before mile marker 200.3—which measures a historic train route that runs from San Bernardino to downtown Los Angeles to south Orange County—Bill Sr. felt the train come to an unplanned stop.

Within a few minutes he called his son to tell him about the delay. But there was no answer, just a recording: "The person you are calling cannot be reached."

He overheard a passenger across the aisle, talking on the phone with her daughter. She said there'd been a death on the tracks.

But Bill Sr. didn't put two and two together.

He had no idea his son had stepped in front of the train he was on.

Bill Sr. and all the other passengers were delayed, many for several hours.

Four other trains also were delayed for varying periods. In all, about 560 people traveling on Metrolink trains in Orange County that evening were forced to take buses to get where they were heading.

The stretch of track where Bill Jr. died didn't reopen until 8:15 p.m., when trains were allowed to travel only at restricted speeds. Even then, cleanup crews still were on the scene. When Bill Sr. finally got to the station in San Juan Capistrano, he got off and carried his luggage through the parking lot, looking for Bill Jr.'s car.

Nothing.

He assumed his son had grown tired of waiting and returned home. He flagged a taxi and went to the Marina Inn in Dana Point. He kept calling, but Bill Jr.'s phone kept repeating the message saying he wasn't available.

Bill Sr. thought his son had taken a sleeping pill. The next morning, at the hotel breakfast, he heard a couple talking about a suicide on the train tracks.

Bill Sr. went back to his room and called the coroner.

At 7:40 a.m. on Oct. 11, the county coroner informed Bill Sr. that Bill Jr. had died after being hit by a Metrolink train.

They'd found a $100 bill, a Visa card, an AAA card and a driver's license, but had checked fingerprints before making a positive I.D.

Like Bill Sr., Kristi had no idea what had happened the evening before. She met with a client that morning and went for a long training walk.

When she checked her phone she had eight messages from her mother-in-law in Texas. Kristi soon called Texas and learned that her husband was dead.

She immediately drove to find Bill Sr.

"As I was driving in the rain to the hotel, my first thought was that this is more than I will ever be able to handle," she said.

"I contemplated slamming my car into the light pole ahead."

At the same time, word was spreading through Dana Point that Bill Brotherton Jr. had stepped in front of a train.

Debbie Preble, the hairdresser who chatted with Bill Jr. outside the bank a day earlier, canceled her appointments. She had been sober for years, but Bill Jr.'s death left her so shaken, she said, that she took to her couch and drank for two weeks.

"I felt responsible," Preble said. "I saw him that morning. I could have done something. I shouldn't have been in a hurry."

That feeling was shared across town.

Dr. Souhail Toubia, who was a workout partner and (because Bill Jr. didn't have health insurance) Bill Jr.'s primary care physician, began questioning himself.

"Why didn't I do something?" Toubia recalls asking himself. "Why didn't I know?"

Another workout partner, Aaron Carlow, couldn't believe the details of his friend's death, particularly the part about Bill Sr. being on the train.

"How could he do that to his father?" Aaron asked.

Guilt and anger are common reactions after suicide—even among people who don't know the person who killed himself, said

Dr. Richard Granese, a psychiatrist who works at several hospitals in Orange County.

And witnessing a graphic death can lead to depression and post-traumatic stress disorder.

Still, Granese stops short of describing a public suicide as a hostile act. He believes a person who commits suicide, even in public, seldom does it for attention or to traumatize witnesses.

"They've gone to place of no return," he said. "They just want to end things."

Bill Sr. refused to say that his boy committed suicide.

In his hotel room, after the coroner told him about Bill Jr., he told Kristi that his son had poor eyesight; that he must have misjudged the approaching train.

Kristi didn't argue.

Helen Shirley, a mail carrier and a longtime friend of Bill Jr., asked if she could keep the giant picture of Bill Jr. that they'd used at his memorial. She placed it at the top of her stairs, next to her father's ashes.

She said Bill Jr. had changed her life for the better with his constant reminders about diet and exercise.

Sometimes, she talks to Bill's photo.

"I say, 'Oh my God, you're an idiot,' " Shirley said. "I hate you so much."

More than a year after his death, the ripple effect hasn't entirely subsided.

Kristi took up public speaking, going to high schools and anyone who would listen to her talk about mental health and how to handle depression. Recently, she became a certified grief counselor.

Kristi said Bill Sr. has never been the same.

He's fallen twice in recent months, and he was unable to continue tending to his goats, so he sold the farm. He cut off his phone service.

"He gave up on life," Kristi said.

Bill Jr. was cremated. His remains are buried at the Evergreen Free Will Baptist Church in Iola, Texas.

In his last interview with the *Register*, Bill Sr. said he visited his son's grave site every 10 days or so.

"I guess I raised him wrong," Bill Sr. said.

Acknowledgments

This book would not have been possible without the editing, generosity, patience, encouragement, and love of Sheila Peterson. You are an amazing friend. I am blessed to have you in my life.

A big thank you to Nikki Nguyen and Cathleen Falsani for the endless conversations and for helping me set the tone and direction of this book.

To Saddleback Church, in particular Pastor James, for encouraging me to write my story of hope, and Rick and Kay Warren for inspiring me to be of service to others and never waste my pain.

To Russell Friedman, co-founder of the Grief Recovery Institute, for his training and guidance.

To my talented and creative editor, Angie Kiesling, for making the editorial process so painless and pleasurable. And a special thank you to Jennifer Grant for lending your poetic eye to my verse.

Thanks to my publisher, Morgan James, for believing in my message.

Thank you to Jack Randall Photography for the beautiful cover shot. Thank you to graphic designer Brooke Davis for my beautiful cover, and Michael Ruffino for not only being a great yoga model but also providing your yogi expertise.

To reporters Keith Sharon, Greg Hardesty, I give you my great thanks for the care and sensitivity you took in telling our story, and for the kind permission of the Orange County Register that allowed me to include your article in this book.

And to my amazing little brother Todd Hugstad and extended family, friends, Pilates and grief clients—thank you for your unconditional love and support.

To my brother, Scott Hugstad-Vaa, my dad, David Hugstad, and my husband, Bill Brotherton—I promise to use the heartache of your deaths to offer hope to anyone who is suffering and in need of tools for navigating grief.

Finally and essentially, to my companion of twenty-one years, Smoke, who went over the Rainbow Bridge in May 2016. Thank you for loving me and Bill with all of your feline heart.

About the Author

For all of Kristi Hugstad's adult life, she had one clear goal: to provide the highest opportunity for fitness and health to everyone who walked into her studio or gym—a feat she accomplished daily for years until the suicide of her husband, Bill Brotherton Jr. In the wake of epic grief, Kristi found a new trajectory. She's made it her mission to reach out to those wrestling with grief and help them confront their pain and fears to gain a new perspective and new life. A resident of Dana Point, California, she is a certified Grief Recovery Specialist, author, speaker, blogger for *The Huffington Post*, and host of *The Grief Girl* radio show and podcast, which can be streamed on iTunes and Podbean. Learn more about Kristi at thegriefgirl.com.